Flowing with Universal Laws

Cosmic Laws, Universal Laws, Subsidiary Laws

By

Margo Kirtikar, Ph.D.

© 2002 by Margo Kirtikar Ph.D. All rights reserved.

No part of this book may be reproduced, stored in a retrieval system, or transmitted by any means, electronic, mechanical, photocopying, recording, or otherwise, without written permission from the author.

ISBN: 1-4033-1683-X (E-book)
ISBN: 1-4033-1684-8 (Paperback)
ISBN: 1-4033-1685-6 (Hardcover)

This book is printed on acid free paper.

Cover Design by Gabrielle von Bernstorff

1stBooks - rev. 07/05/02

to my grandson

rafael

Introduction

The Tales of the Arabian Nights, the One thousand and One Nights, are revelations of Divine Laws and are much more than folklore for children and adults, when the tales are truly and correctly understood. The inner implications of accomplishments are perfectly possible when one is sincere, worthy and humble enough to be trusted with the power and the truth that they reveal. The great master 'ignorance' and his close friends 'pride, doubt, fear, ridicule, skepticism' and many of such useless parasites, have fastened themselves upon the mentality and feeling of humans making them blind, holding them slaves within their own self imposed limitations. If it were not for these negative traits which act like vampires, mankind would be able to see and to know that within the light that animates the physical body, exists an intelligence and a power that can and will carry out perfectly whatever the mind directs. This can be done when harmony is maintained and all that is thought and aspired for is of a constructive nature.

'In Him we live and move and have our Being.' The cosmic energy in which we bathe surrounds us so we can say that we live in God's energy. Cosmic Law rules everything in the cosmos and Universal Law rules everything on earth. Cosmic and Universal Laws are spiritual and, therefore, invisible, unchangeable and eternal. These laws make our world what it is. The laws manifest themselves through energy and we humans have been given the freedom, the intelligence and the will power to activate these energies and to make them work for us. But in order to activate these laws, we need to be aware of them and we need to understand them. The more we are able to integrate attributes of universal laws into our daily lives the more harmony we have in our life and we experience what we refer to as 'going with the flow.' When we live against the energies of these laws of nature we experience a disharmony in our life where everything seems to go wrong for us. We have been given the freedom of choice, to do one or the other, to work with or against these invisible laws. We all know deep inside us of the existence of these spiritual laws, if we would only take a moment to listen in silence to the spirit within. It is never too late to study universal laws, to contemplate and to understand them the best way we can. It is never too late to apply them in our daily life so that we can make things change for the better in our world. Any moment can be the right moment to begin. The universal laws assure us of that.

Contents

Introduction v
Who we are 1
Universal Laws transcend all Religions..................................5
'As above so below.' 8
The Constitution of the Universe 11
Universal Laws...12
The Law of the Absolute 25
The Law of Abstraction 26
The Law of Abundance 28
The Law of Acceptance 30
The Law of Accommodation 31
The Law of Action...32
The Law of Action and Reaction...33
The Law of Activity 34
The Law of Adaptation 35
The Law of Adjustment..36
The Law of Affection 37
The Law of Affinity...38
The Law of Akasha 40
The Law of the Alpha and Omega..41
The Law of Analogy 42
The Law of Archetype 44
The Law of Ascension 45
The Law of Assembly 46
The Law of Attraction...47

The Law of Attraction and Repulsion 48
The Law of Authority 51
The Law of Averages 52
The Law of Awareness 53
The Law of Balance 54
The Law of Being 56
The Law of Believing and Knowing 58
The Law of Challenge 59
The Law of Change 60
The Law of Chemical Affinity 62
The Law of Co-creation 63
The Law of Choice 64
The Law of Circulation/Circle 65
The Law of Coalescence 66
The Law of Cohesion 67
The Law of Color 68
The Law of Common Ground 70
The Law of Communication 71
The Law of Compassion 72
The Law of Compensation 73
The Law of Completion 75
The Law of Concentration 76
The Law of Condensing Light 77
The Law of Consciousness 79
The Law of Continuity of Consciousness 81
The Law of Correlation 82
The Law of Cosmic Equation 83

The Law of Cosmic Manifestation 84
The Law of Courage 85
The Law of Creativity 86
The Law of Credibility 88
The Law of Cycles 89
The Law of Cyclic Returns 90
The Law of Description 92
The Law of Desire 93
The Law of Destiny 94
The Law of Dharma 95
The Law of Differentiation 96
The Law of Discipline 98
The Law of Disintegration 99
The Law of Dissolution 101
The Law of Divine Flow 102
The Law of Divine Union 103
The Law of Drama 104
The Law of Duality 105
The Law of the Earth 107
The Law of Economy 109
The Law of Economy of Force 110
The Law of Education 111
The Law of Elevation 113
The Law of Energy 114
The Law of Enthusiasm 115
The Law of Essence 117
The Law of Essential Integrity 118

The Law of Evolution	119
The Law of Example	121
The Law of Exclusion	122
The Law of Expansion	123
The Law of Expectation	125
The Law of Faith	126
The Law of Fixation	127
The Law of Flexibility	128
The Law of Forgiveness	129
The Law of Freedom	131
The Law of Free Will	133
The Law of Friction	134
The Law of Fulfillment	135
The Law of Garment of Light	136
The Law of Gender	137
The Law of Giving	138
The Law of Goodness	140
The Law of Goodwill	141
The Law of Grace	143
The Law of Gratitude	144
The Law of Gravitation	145
The Law of Group Endeavor	146
The Law of Group Life	147
The Law of Group Progress	148
The Law of Growth	149
The Law of Happiness	150
The Law of Harmony	151

The Law of Healing	152
The Law of Higher Will	154
The Law of Honesty	155
The Law of Honor	156
The Law of Humility	157
The Law of Identity	158
The Law of Impartiality	159
The Law of Increase	160
The Law of Inertia	162
The Law of Infinite Energy	163
The Law of Infinity	165
The Law of Initiation	166
The Law of Initiative	169
The Law of Integration	170
The Law of Intelligence	171
The Law of Intention	172
The Law of Interdependence	173
The Law of Intuition	174
The Law of Isolation/Limitation	175
The Law of Inverse Proportions	176
The Law of Justice	177
The Sirian Law of Karma	179
The Law of Knowledge	182
The Law of Least Effort	184
The Law of Leverage	185
The Law of Liability	186
The Law of Liberation	187

The Law of Life	188
The Law of Light	190
The Law of Love	192
The Law of Lotus	194
The Law of Macrocosm and Microcosm	196
The Law of Magic	197
The Law of Magnetic Control	198
The Law of Magnetic Impulse	199
The Law of Magnetism	200
The Law of Manifestation	201
The Law of Mantras	203
The Law of Meditation	205
The Law of Meekness	208
The Law of Mentalism	209
The Law of Mercy	210
The Law of Miracles	211
The Law of Moderation	212
The Law of Monadic Return	213
The Law of Money	214
The Law of Non-intervention	215
The Law of Non-Judgement	216
Law of Non-Resistance	217
The Law of Number Measure and Weight	220
The Law of One	221
The Law of Opportunity	222
The Law of Order and Creation	223
The Law of Paradox	224

The Law of Patience	226
The Law of Patterns	227
The Law of Peace	228
The Law of Penetration	230
The Law of Perception	231
The Law of Perfection	232
The Law of Periodicity	233
The Law of Permanence	234
The Law of Perspective	235
The Law of Planetary Affinity	236
The Law of Planning	238
The Law of Polarity	239
The Law of Poverty	240
The Law of Practice	241
The Law of Praise	242
The Law of Prayer and Meditation	244
The Law of Present Moment	246
The Law of Privacy	247
The Law of Process	248
The Law of Productivity	249
The Law of Progress	250
The Law of Projection	251
The Law of Prophecy	252
The Law of Prosperity	253
The Law of Purification	255
The Law of Radiation	256
The Law of Reality	257

The Law of Rebirth	258
The Law of Rebound	260
The Law of Receiving	261
The Law of Reconciliation	263
The Law of Reflection	264
The Law of Reincarnation	265
The Law of Relativity	266
The Law of Relaxation	267
The Law of Release	268
The Law of Repetition	269
The Law of Repulse	270
The Law of Repulsion	271
The Law of Respect	272
The Law of Respiration	273
The Law of Responsibility	275
The Law of Revelation	276
The Law of Rhythm	277
The Law of Right Human Relations	279
The Law of Right to one's Space	280
The Law of Ritual and Ceremony	281
The Law of Sacrifice	282
The Law of Sacrifice and Death	284
The Law of Schools	285
The Law of Security	286
The Law of Service	287
The Law of Sex	288
The Law of Silence	289

The Law of Simplicity	290
The Law of Solar Evolution	291
The Law of Solar Union	292
The Law of Soul	293
The Law of Sound	295
The Law of Speech	298
The Law of Spiral Movement	300
The Law of Spirit	301
The Law of Spiritual Approach	302
The Law of Spiritual Awakening	303
The Law of Spiritual Non Perfection	304
The Law of the Subconscious Mind	305
The Law of Substitution	306
The Law of Suggestion	307
The Law of Summons	308
The Law of Supply	309
The Law of Surrender	311
The Law of Symbols	312
The Law of Synthesis	314
The Law of Teaching	315
The Law of Telepathy	317
The Law of Tenfold Return	318
The Law of Thought	319
The Law of Three	321
The Law of Three Requests	323
The Law of Time	324
The Law of Tolerance	325

The Law of Truth	326
The Law of Unconditional Love	327
The Law of Unfulfillment	328
The Law of Unity	329
The Law of Unity and Separation	330
The Law of Universal Sympathy	331
The Law of Vacuum	332
The Law of Vibration	333
The Law of Will of God	335
The Law of Will Power	336
The Law of Wisdom	337
The Soul's Journey	338
Afterword	341
Glossary	345
Bibliography	353

Who we are

To truly know who we are we need to understand our complete human identity, our origin, our direction, our purpose and our duty as humans. Through self-knowledge we can create a state of health in which our spiritual and physical resources are equally active and in balance working in harmony towards a common goal.

We are created as multi dimensional beings to experience life and to manifest our true nature and essence, the spirit, through a physical form. Our original home is in the spiritual dimension. Our purpose here on earth as we complete our human journey back to the spiritual dimension, is to develop, to strengthen and to refine our human qualities. We are meant to evolve in the physical world because the conditions in the tangible world are non existent on the spiritual realm. In other words imagine the earth as being our school and playground and through each of our earth life we are going through a specific training in order to evolve. The challenge is for us to progress and to refine our character while being completely involved in the physical world, using our physical senses. Our challenge is that as we go through our earth life, we are meant to remember our spiritual identity and origin.

Being the dominant species on earth, we are entrusted with the responsibility of being the guardians of the three lower kingdoms, the mineral, the plant and the animal worlds. Both our internal state of being and our external behavior and actions affect all life on our planet. If our world is out of balance, as we are experiencing now, it is because something has gone wrong within us. We have created a crisis in our relationships with all forms of life on earth and no amount of science or technology can correct this imbalance. Both the problem and the solution relate to our individual and collective state of being. None of what we humanity are experiencing now are acts of nature or done unto us by God. The destruction of our environment, our competitive and materialistic behavior, the poverty, the social injustice, crime, wars, exploitation of natural resources, are all symptoms of the huge imbalance in our own human nature and our development. We humanity, collectively, have no one to blame for all of our misfortunes but ourselves. We are the cause of our misery.

The chaos and the suffering that we presently experience is the terrible price that we must pay for breaking the laws of nature and the universe and for neglecting our spiritual faculties causing a disparity within us. Granted we have made gigantic progress in scientific and technological knowledge in the past century but in the meantime, we have sadly also created a chaotic world. The only way to correct this is if we change our individual and collective state of consciousness. To the average human, life is an enigma, a deep mystery, a complex and an incomprehensible puzzle. But mystery is only another name for ignorance and everything that is unknown and not understood is a mystery. Once we understand, what once appeared to be mysterious, is suddenly no mystery any more. Therefore, it is knowledge plus the understanding that is the key to the puzzle and the mystery of life.

The human is a creature of constant growth living in a boundless ocean of progress to be discovered and conquered by developing and cultivating one's inborn powers. The progress of the individual is mainly determined by the ruling mental powers that regulate one's actions and direction of one's faculties and powers, the sum total of which determine each one's personal fate. The ruling state of mind that is adopted by the individual is in accordance with the experiences and perception of the events in one's life. If one's predominant state of mind and attitudes are broadminded, harmonious, positive and aspiring then all energy will be directed towards constructive channels. If, however, one's disposition is negative, uncontrolled and disharmonious then all forces will be misdirected. Nature has no problems because she is orderly and disciplined and so when we have a problem, it is simply because we are not cooperating with a law of Nature or the Cosmos.

Many of us today in the more 'civilized' part of the world suffer from a particular disease, namely an over developed intellect. Our mental activity dominates our inner feelings. While thinking is necessary and valuable to organize, to plan and to structure our life, it is an incomplete way to experience our life because we experience only a part and not the whole. Our thoughts must be coordinated with our inner feelings because it is through our feelings that we identify our human needs and those of other life forms. The other 'malheur' that many of us suffer from is our neglect of the spirit within and this has created a vacuum within our being. We have managed to fill this vacuum with an over stimulated intellect and we have the tendency to think rather than feel our way through life. Unless we can balance our thinking with our feelings, intellect and heart, to be sensitive to our needs and to the needs of others, we reduce ourselves to being materialists, competitive, inconsiderate and egoistic. It is this vacuum that is now actually experienced as a deep empty hole in the chest area. It is this ache that we now desperately try to rid ourselves of, as we turn our attention to find solace in spirituality. We

Margo Kirtikar Ph.D.

have finally realized that the material world is not the answer to everything and we are beginning to think that there might just be something else out there beyond our physical world.

Universal Laws transcend all Religions

The nature of spirit is an individual philosophy for each and every one of us. No matter how diverse our beliefs or philosophies are, we in the physical world are all bound together by our thoughts, feelings, dreams, aspirations and actions. Universal laws are the basic principles of life, which transcend the diversity of individual beliefs. These Laws apply to whatever our belief system or philosophy is. When applied correctly the universal laws allow us to reach our maximum spiritual potential and greatly enhance the experience of our manifestation in the material world. Understanding universal laws enables us to review and see why our life is the way it is, where we might have gone wrong and how we can amend things.

Various Prophets were sent throughout the ages to all corners of the world to spread God's teachings to people of different cultures and tongues. Each of the Prophets and their disciples, some well known others less known and long forgotten, carried a particular message from the Higher Powers, the Source, God, suitable to that particular time and in accordance to the needs of the masses. These teachings eventually developed into the many religions and beliefs that are existent today. If we make an in-depth study of the essence of each of these teachings, however, we would find a great similarity and a common thread running through all the disciplines. In fact we find all religions to be basically the same in essence. The theme of loving and honoring one another is the foundation for all alike. Any differences of opinions found in religions are usually misinterpretations of the truth, and these distortions have been imposed and forced upon the minds of the people by ignorant, evil, power-hungry men with one intention only in mind: to keep the masses under their control through fear.

The essence in all religions talks of non violence and ethical values, truth and purity, justice, control of the senses, honoring our parents and treating all other living beings as we would treat ourselves. Following are some examples:

'A man should wander about treating all creatures as he himself would be treated.' Jainism. Stutrakritanga 1.11.33.

'Not one of you is a believer until he loves for his brother what he loves for himself.' Islam. Forty Hadith of an-Nawawi 13.

'You shall love thy neighbor as thyself.' Judaism and Christianity Bible, Leviticus 19.18.

'Whatever you wish that men would do to you, do so to them.' Christianity. Bible, Matthew 7.12.

'One should not behave towards others in a way which is disagreeable to oneself. This is the essence of morality. All other activities are due to selfish desire.' Hinduism, Mahabharata, Anusasana Parva, 113.8.

'Try your best to treat others as you would wish to be treated yourself, and you will find that this the shortest way to benevolence.' Chinese. Confucianism. Mencius VII.A.4.

'One to take a pointed stick to kill a bird should first try it on himself to feel how it hurts.' (African Traditional Religion. Proverb Nigeria.)

'Whatever affliction may visit you is for what your own hands have earned.' Islam. Qur'an 42.30.

'Suffering is the offspring of violence. Realize this and be watchful.' Jainism. Acarangasutra 3.13.

'Our body in Kali Yuga is a field of action, as man sows, so is his reward. Nothing is determined by empty talk. Anyone swallowing poison must die. Brother, behold the Creator's justice, as are a man's actions, so is his recompense.' Sikhism, Adi Granth, Guri Var, M.4, p.308.

'All who take the sword will perish by the sword.' Christiniaty, Bible, Matthew 26.52.

'Ashes fly back in the face of him who throws them.' African Traditional Religions.Yoruba Proverb Nigeria.

'Unrighteousness practiced in this world, does not at once produce its fruit, but like a cow, advancing slowly, it cuts off the roots of him who committed it.' Hinduism, Laws of Manu. 4. 172.

'Men who acquire wealth by evil deeds, by adhering to principles which are wrong, fall into the trap of their own passions and fettered with karma they sink further down.' Jainism. Uttaradyayana Sutra 4.2.

'As you plan for somebody so God plans for you.' African Traditional Religions. Igbo Proverb Nigeria.

The following passage is perhaps the most significant because it refers clearly to the energies of Cosmic and Universal Laws that one cannot escape.

'Not in the sky, nor in mid-ocean, nor in a mountain cave, is found that place on earth where abiding one may escape from the consequences of one's evil deed.' Buddhism. Dhammapada 127.

The God Almighty is referred to as the all seeing that one cannot hide from. Today we have the intelligence and understanding to realize that the 'All Seeing God' and the 'Cosmic and Universal Laws or Energies' are one and the same.

Margo Kirtikar Ph.D.

'As above so below.'

Hermes Trismegistus said: 'That which is below is like to that which is above.' Some people erroneously believe this to mean that what is on earth is the same as it is in Heaven, the macro-micro cosmic relation. In fact, what is actually meant here was that life on earth is subjected to the same Cosmic Laws that the Higher Spheres are subjected to.

Modern science is well versed in physics and chemistry. However, modern science does not as yet fully accept the existence of spiritual physics or spiritual chemistry, or the psychic world as governed by moral laws. Granted it is not always easy to identify these laws but that is no reason to claim that they do not exist. An invisible world does exist and our whole life, if we really stop to think about it is based on things we cannot see. More and more we are becoming aware of the fact that our inner world is governed by a non-physical world. Even if you do not believe in God you cannot fail to recognize that there is an order in nature and consequently, there must be a Higher Intelligence which created that order.

Initiatic Science acknowledges the existence of three worlds: the divine world which is the level of ideas, the psychic world which is the level of thoughts and feelings, and the physical world, the world of forms and materialism. Just as we earthlings have to obey nature's laws, nature obeys the laws of the Spirit and it is Spirit that commands nature. The material world in which we live is linked to the 'moral' world, which in turn is linked to the far higher world of ideas. Because these moral laws are not written down on paper, some people think that they have the right to do whatever they want but ignorance is no defense before the law. Even if we do not know of these unwritten moral laws, those who fail to abide by these laws inevitably pay the high price of remorse, suffering, bitterness, disappointments and sometimes they might even have to pay the price for their folly with money or with their life. More and more we begin to understand that everything in life is connected and related to everything else, so one can never act alone and think it does not concern anyone else. In fact what each one of us thinks and does very much concerns and touches everyone else in some fashion or another, in the short term or the long term.

For us to have a contented and joyful life we must recognize and accept three major laws: Universal Laws, Moral Laws and Human laws. The same laws are at work on all levels of existence for the Universe is one and on every level and at every stage the same phenomena can be found, although always in different more subtle forms. Our Earth is a living being, it breathes and grows and changes constantly. It is said that nature has a memory and nothing can ever erase what it has once recorded. Whatever we find on earth can be found also in water, and whatever is in water exists in air and in all living things. All four elements of nature obey the same laws with some differences in the way they apply the laws. Some react violently and others rapidly. For instance the human mind is analogous to the element air, and this is expressed in the form of ideas and thoughts. Emotions are analogous to the element water and these can be either abysmal, dismal and cumbrous or pure, virtuous and light.

Over and above the physical body, the human has subtle bodies: etheric, astral, mental, causal, buddhic and atmic. The tragic reality is that most of us are ignorant of our own structure and composition and of the constant interaction that goes on between human beings and the invisible beings in the other regions of the universe. It is this ignorance which is the cause of all our misfortunes. It is easy to create the future but it is very difficult to erase the past. Good always produces good and evil always produces evil. Some people might think that if one is too kind one can get hurt or if one is too generous one gets taken advantage of. This is in reality selfish thinking. The truth is we can never be too kind, too generous, too loving or too considerate towards others. The universe created by God is an immense world bursting with treasures in great abundance. How can we go wrong if we live in abundance following the guidance of the Higher Intelligence that has so marvelously ordered and arranged such a miraculous abundant beautiful world.

The Constitution of the Universe

In recent decades, modern science has systematically revealed deeper layers of order in Nature, from the atomic to the nuclear and sub-nuclear level of Nature's functioning. This progressive exploration has culminated in the recent discovery of the Unified Field of all the laws of Nature the ultimate source of order in the Universe.

Both modern and ancient understandings, locate the unified source of Nature's perfect order in a single, self-interacting field of intelligence at the foundation of all the laws of Nature. This field consecutively creates, from within itself, all the diverse laws of Nature governing life at every level of the manifest Universe. The Unified Field of Natural law inside and its diversified expression outside are completely parallel to each other. The laws governing the self-interacting dynamics of the unified field are the eternal non-changing basis of natural law and the ultimate source of the order and harmony that is displayed throughout creation.

It is written in ancient scriptures that the laws of Nature are imposed upon humanity and cannot be avoided. If these laws are broken, infringed or side stepped, they carry their own penalty within themselves, and this nemesis cannot be avoided. This gives us a sense of justice as we create our own heaven or hell here on earth.

Universal Laws

Universal laws are unbreakable, unchangeable principles of life that operate inevitably, in all phases of our life and existence, for all human beings and all life, everywhere, all the time. Science attempts to unravel the mysteries of our solar system as it pursues a definite course, operating by a technique of intelligent control for both physical and spiritual forces. This unraveling when clearly understood become laws. To name a few of the laws that we are familiar with: The laws of Gravity, the laws of Mathematics, the laws of Physics, the laws of Chemistry, the laws of Electricity and the laws of Thermodynamics. These laws reflect the principles of how the mysteries of physical life unfold. While scientists focus on unraveling physical mysteries, those people who encompass many different belief systems focus on the laws of a spiritual nature.

Universal laws act as guidelines to define the order and structure of creation. They are universal because they apply to all life, any time and any place. Because we all have minds and our minds are designed to work for us, each one of us has the ability to create our heart's desires by cooperating with the universal laws. It does not matter what field of endeavor we pursue, in science, music, media, art, business, religion, politics, communication or relationships. Thought control is the key to destiny and in order to learn thought control we have to know and understand these laws.

Universal laws do not discriminate. The same principles work for all alike. These laws can work for you or against you whether you are aware of them or not. You do not have to believe in the laws for them to work. Knowing about and understanding the universal laws and cooperating with them with awareness, however, will make you more effective in all your endeavors. When you comply with universal laws you will be able to create higher and greater achievements while you expend less energy and direct it more efficiently. You will be investing your mental, emotional and physical energy wisely because you will be able to produce what you desire with the minimum of effort.

The universe is an orderly place, in spite of the chaos we observe on earth at times. All forms of life and all actions that occur in the universe are governed by universal laws. Minerals, animals and the vegetative worlds live in accordance with the laws of the Universe. We humans are the only species who are arrogant enough to think that we are clever and powerful enough to override the laws of nature. For our childish foolishness we are presently experiencing the results all around us on every level. Every plant, animal, human and material object have their own needs that must be satisfied if we are all to experience a life of balance and harmony equally. It is our responsibility as the earth's guardians to honor and support these needs. The higher universal laws are laws of transformation. As we apply each of these laws to an aspect of our life, we begin to change the nature of our life from what it is today to what we hope it can be in the future. Sometimes, long struggles and suffering is inevitable to force changes in order to flow with universal laws. It took, for example, struggle, courage, resistance and going against established human laws in order to end slavery and apartheid.

Cosmic and universal laws are described in Holy Scriptures of all religions, in mythology, in fairy tales, in business success literature, and allegories that describe the essence and nature of man. They are natural laws, mental laws, physical laws and spiritual laws all at the same time. They apply to all life forms, all matter and spirit, in all places and at all times. They are the same for all beliefs, all religions, all cultures. Sir Isaac Newton, Albert Einstein and many other famous individuals, who have contributed to mankind, became familiar with some of these eternal truths. We may know some of them as simple truths, eternal principals, philosophies for living, etc. but when we examine them more closely and experience them we will recognize them as divine laws.

One spiritual Master gives us a definition of a universal law: "Law is the will of the seven Deities, making its impression upon substance in order to produce a specific intent through the method of the evolutionary process." The seven Deities referred to are the seven Lords or Rays of Energy with their seven individual qualities that govern over the Cosmos, through whom, manifests the will of the Creator. These are the Ray of Will Power, the Ray of Love and Wisdom, the Ray of Active Intelligence, the Ray of Harmony through Conflict, the Ray of Scientific Knowledge, the Ray of Idealism and Devotion, and the Ray of Organization and Ceremonial Order. Everything on earth is influenced by the qualities of these ray energies.

Everything in the universe is scientific and is mathematically perfect down to the minute detail, there is law and order everywhere and a reason for everything. In everything and in every circumstance is the reign of law. The Universal laws rule on every plane of being and every grade is under the same laws. The operation of laws can be easily understood. What we need to understand absolutely is that it is we who activate a law of the Universe through our thoughts and actions individually and collectively. The law does not operate itself. As we have been given the freedom of choice, we can make right or wrong choices. We have at the same time been given the choice to correct our mistakes. When we break one law, therefore, and we repent, we have been given the opportunity to take an alternative action and to put things right again. We do this by activating another law.

Before delving further into specific universal laws, here are some excerpts from various ancient scriptures and manuscripts on universal laws:

"In all space there is one pulse and the law of Cosmos is one for all that exists. All things are interrelated. Everything gains nourishment from the same source, Prana (Energy or Spiritus Mundi) *the manifested Power of Cosmos. Cosmic manifestations are limitless. Cosmos the Builder and its reflection, the microcosm, live by the same law. Nothing is wasted by Cosmos and the reserve is guarded. There is no lull in the Cosmos. All is permeated with ceaseless currents. Death is a life generating exchange through realization of the Law of Exchange. Exchange of energies. The interchange of substances and energies is without end. The interchange is manifested in the striving in Cosmos toward perfection.*

Human is the highest manifestation of Cosmos. He is chosen as the predestined builder and collector of all treasures of the universe. The centers of Cosmos are identical with the centers (the seven major chakras) of man. Man bears within himself all manifestations of Cosmos. The interrelation between all Cosmic forces and man has been attested by most ancient revelations. Man is part of the cosmic energy, part of the elements, part of Cosmic Reason, and part of consciousness of the higher matter.

The universal energy relates to all that exists hence, the differentiation between material and immaterial shows ignorance. The existing power of energy can be asserted in the whole of Cosmos. Matter is not applicable as an independent force, because active energies are needed for manifestation. Similarly, energies are needed to propel life. These are called movers of the essence. In Cosmos lives that power of reason, which is called the cosmic rhythm, and the whole of human life depends on the cycles of this rhythm. Accidental shifting do not occur, nor does destruction occur without a possibility of an evident restitution.

The theory, which affirms that life is not moved by a conscious vital impulse, reveals the loss of the most precious meaning and life becomes void of spirit and its creativeness. A limited consciousness attracts only imperfect currents. The power of creativeness responds to the call of the spirit. Why should one limit the Cosmos to earth alone in the belief that Cosmos provided only the one refuge to man? Knowledge of the functions of elements of the universe in relation to the organism of man will make of us cosmic co-workers. Man determines his own destination in Cosmos. In the kernel of the spirit a dissociated atom carries the knowledge of its destiny. Only that spirit (human) *who guards the kernel and keeps it ablaze can affirm his true destiny.*

The beauty of Cosmos is manifested in silence. The beauty of silence is expressed in all the higher manifestations of life. The transmission of thought is also a manifestation of silence. Cosmos proclaims that life pulsates in all atoms and sets into motion the process of evolution. Cosmos proclaims not only the organic but also all manifestations. It proclaims psycho life. Psycho dynamics of the spirit constitutes the foundation of being. Psycho vision is the basis of sight. In all cosmic manifestations we perceive psycho life. The psycho life activates the atom, and the atomic energy is the lever of psycho life of the atom. The principle of human life emerges from the psycho life of the atom. All cells demonstrate not only the process of growth but also the existing psycho dynamics of Cosmos. Humans also reveal the same psycho dynamics diffused throughout the Cosmos. When those who know the principle of psycho dynamics will realize that, then access to the cosmic energy may be gained. People who circumscribe themselves by the evident and who sense only the obvious limit their world. The highest perception is accessible only to the one who knows the spiritual world. Psychic energy opens all gates. The spiritual world is without bounds; and the physical mind cannot manifest the knowledge of infinity. Only the psycho dynamic power of spirit carries man into the higher spheres. The limitless vision opens the paths to the Heart of the Cosmos.

The task of humanity is to establish the harmony of existence and the creativeness of the infinite Cosmos. In Cosmos there is a most gigantic equilibrium and the power of equilibrium is maintained through a harmonized psycho life. The beauty of life is in the affirmation of multi formity. Cosmos does not favor uniformity. Cosmos is diffused in the consciousness of billions of forms. The limitation of consciousness is death to the spirit. The mightiest lever of Cosmos and the most sacred is the heart, only through the heart can we discern the beauty of the world manifested by the heart of the Cosmos. By the way of the heart we can penetrate into the consciousness of the Cosmic breath. The heart was always considered as the symbol of the guiding one and life expands by that symbol.

The rebirth of a country is always created through cosmic influences. The agglomeration of propelled thoughts attracts from space the necessary layers of manifested sending. Clichés of great discoveries float in space. Those who can intensify their psychic energy with the rhythm of cosmic energies will absorb the cosmic treasures into their consciousness. The broadening of consciousness will propel toward the chain, which connects all creative forces of

Margo Kirtikar Ph.D.

Cosmos. Man cannot isolate himself from the entire cosmic process, as an independent unit."

The message is clear and simple. The law of the Cosmos is one for all and all things are interrelated, nothing can exist independent of anything else. Matter and spirit, therefore, are interdependent and one cannot exist without the other. The interchange of all creation is infinite always striving for perfection. All gain nourishment from the one Essence. Cosmic manifestations are limitless and nothing is wasted, everything is correlated. The human being the highest manifestation of the Cosmos is a Co-creator. It is through the psycho dynamic power of spirit that we are able to contact the Higher Spheres and the golden key is thought control. The Cosmos thrives on boundless opulence and billions of varieties of forms. The Cosmos, therefore, does not favor limitations or uniformity and this idea makes us realize just how ludicrous we are when we seek uniformity in our lives, on any level, or when we imagine one to be better than the other because of race, color, shape or size. The whole of human life depends on the cycles of the cosmic rhythm and there are no such things as accidents while we experience the ebb and flow in everything that passes. Above all the beauty of the Cosmos is manifested in the language of silence.

It is through expanding our consciousness and intensifying our psychic energy to be in harmony with the cosmic rhythm, that we are able to enter the Cosmic Silence, gain contact with the creative forces of Cosmos and absorb some of the treasures into our consciousness. Every artist, writer, musician, inventor, architect, leader and all creative people in every field on every level, whose work has transformed human consciousness and inspired humanity over a longer period of time, have used this method with or without awareness.

According to ancient teaching there are three fundamental laws of the Cosmos of the greater system, recognized by astronomers of which we form a part. Subsidiary to the three major laws are the seven laws of our solar system. An intermediate law known as the law of Karma is the synthetic law of the system of Sirius.

1) The Three Cosmic Laws
    The law of Synthesis
    The law of Attraction and Repulsion
    The law of Economy of Force

2) The Sirian law of Karma.

3) The Seven laws of the Solar System.

These seven laws concern the form side of life. These are the basis of all true psychological understanding and when we can comprehend their influence, we will eventually arrive at real self-knowledge.

   The law of Vibration
   The law of Cohesion
   The law of Disintegration
   The law of Magnetic Control
   The law of Fixation
   The law of Love
   The law of Sacrifice

There are hundreds of subsidiary universal laws and principles, some clear and simple to understand others complex, paradox and oxymoron. It is up to each one of us to gather our own understanding of each law and to apply this according to our own state of mind and state of affairs at any one moment in our life. We need to keep in mind that these laws exist in order for the world to function with efficiency, and that we have been given the privilege of the will to activate these energies, for better or worse with intelligence. The same law might be right in one situation but wrong in another situation. We are given the freedom to discriminate and to make choices. There is a Sufi parable known as the 'Tale of the Sands' which reflects on this issue.

A bubbling stream reached a desert and found it difficult to cross. The water was disappearing into the fine sand faster and faster so the Stream spoke to the Desert: 'My destiny is to cross this desert but I don't know how to.'

The voice of the desert answered in the hidden tongue of nature and said: 'If the Wind crosses the desert so can you.'

'But whenever I try, I am absorbed into the sand and even if I dash myself at the desert, I can go only a little distance.'

The desert voice answered quietly, 'The wind does not dash itself against the desert sand.'

'But the wind can fly and I cannot fly.'

'You are thinking in the wrong way, trying to fly by yourself is absurd. You are water. Allow the wind to carry you over the sand.'

The stream said: 'But how can that happen?'

'Allow yourself to be absorbed in the wind.'

The stream protested that it did not want to lose its individuality in that way. If it did, it might not exist again.

This, said the sand, was a form of logic, but it did not refer to reality at all. When the wind absorbs moisture, it carries it over the desert, and then lets it fall again like rain and the rain again becomes a river again.

But how, asked the stream, could it know that this was true?

'It is so and you must believe it, or you will simply be sucked down by the sands to form, after several million years a quagmire.'

'But if this is so, will I be the same river that I am today?'

'You cannot in any case remain the same stream that you are today. The choice is not open to you; it only seems to be open. The wind will carry your essence, the finer part of you. When you become a river again at the mountains beyond the sands, men may call you by a different name; but you yourself, essentially, will know that you are the same. Today you call yourself such and such a river only because you do not know which part of it is even now your essence.'

So the stream crossed the desert by raising itself into the arms of the welcoming wind, which gathered it slowly and carefully upward and then let it down with gentle firmness, atop the mountains of a far off land. 'Now,' said the stream, 'I have learned my true identity.'

But the stream had a question, which it bubbled up as it sped along: 'Why could I not reason this out on my own? Why did the sands have to tell me? What would have happened if I had not listened to the sands?'

Suddenly a small voice spoke to the stream. It came from a grain of sand. 'Only the sands know, for they have seen it happen; moreover, they extend from the river to the mountain. They form the link and they have their function to perform, as has everything in the universe. The way in which the stream of life is to carry itself on its journey is written in the Sands.'

Cosmic Laws
Universal Laws
Subsidiary Laws

Margo Kirtikar Ph.D.

The Law of the Absolute

Universal laws are absolute and non negotiable. No soul stands outside universal law and ignorance of the law is no excuse. The Absolute is above all that exists. Who are we to argue with that? We have no choice but to accept this as it is.

Margo Kirtikar Ph.D.

The Law of Abstraction

This law concerns the ability to create through higher abstract thoughts. To arrive to this level we need to master the art of abstract thinking and we need to have gone through the painful lessons of detachment. To achieve the state of detachment it is necessary to relinquish all attachment to relationships and material forms and what more it is necessary to do this willingly. Detachment does not mean giving up all one's earthly possessions. It merely means not to be a slave to the material world of possessions and a slave to one's emotions. It is through this law that one is lifted, out of the human plane, in an upward drive which all units of life express, in search for identification with the Divine. The entire process of abstraction is involved with pain. The words to meditate on here are: detachment, liberation, rejection, relinquishment, renunciation, withdrawal, negation, abstraction—OM.

A good place to start is to work with mental power training exercises, 'mind over matter' following the Yoga Sutras of the Indian Sage Pantajali. Since the training is quite rigorous it is important to cultivate a happy spirit during the training. Neither loneliness nor depression should bring one down, two qualities that one is sure to experience during the training. One should not dwell on the horrors of the world but meditate instead to convey strength and wisdom. This teaches one to keep the lower emotions in check since spreading emotions such as pity, sadness, criticism, helplessness are negative and detrimental to the Spirit and to the world. So by concentrating on the positive such as strength and wisdom and active intelligence, one spreads these energies into the atmosphere instead. In order to be a co-Creator on a higher level you need to master the ability of abstract thinking. With abstract thought one is able to have a bird's eye view of everything. Imagination and creativity might require some years of practice for some who are better at linear thinking. For others abstract thought, imagination and creativity comes naturally. Do not make the mistake of comparing yourself with others, just follow your own inner prompting and do what seems right for you and appropriate to your circumstances at any one time. Widening one's horizon and mind, changing one's habits and stepping out of ones own limitations, usually involves discomfort and suffering at first, but the transformation in consciousness and the rewards that follow make it worthwhile. See also the law of Creativity.

Margo Kirtikar Ph.D.

The Law of Abundance

This law is also known as the law of Opulence. If we look around us we see nothing but abundance of everything in our world. Everything comes in a multitude of varieties. Whether its colors, animals, fruits, plants, trees or humans and we are all meant to enjoy and share in this world of abundance. Just look at the variety of colors that we see in the animal world, birds and fish for example, or the variety of types and colors of the flower family or the vegetable and fruit world. Every one flower and fruit gives us one or several more seeds to plant even more of the same kind. Look at the variety of humans, shapes, colors and sizes. Listen to the varieties of music of all cultures and marvel at the fact that all music is based on seven basic major tones. Abundance is everywhere around us. We ought to accept this as a state of affairs and to connect to all the opulence, because we harbor this abundance in us as well, we can manifest this in our life if we are able to learn to escape from our self imposed limitations. If we humans feel any limitations anywhere or at any time in our life this is caused by none other than ourselves, through our own false beliefs and values, through our fears, selfishness and greed.

We can create abundance in our lives by first believing in ourselves, and then to care about everything that we love in our life. The key is not to focus on one area only shutting out or neglecting everything else in our life. We need to be aware at every stage of all our thoughts and all our multi layered actions. Our mind has the capacity of producing exactly what we expect from it. According to what we think we can either live in a world of abundance and joy or we can live in a small limited sad world. We are given the choice. We create our world with our mind so if we wish to have an abundance of anything in our lives all we need to do is to change our thoughts. It is through a well trained and developed mind that we are able to control and to change our thoughts. Like ebb and flow there is also a time for abundance and a time for holding back, a time for overflow and fullness and a time of emptiness. It is left up to us to be sensitive to our own needs, the energies surrounding us, creating the rhythm of our individual lives. When we create an image of abundance in our life we draw this energy of success and opulence into our reality and the success and abundance here does not apply to money only. One can have success in all aspects of one's life, in one's relationships, spirituality, knowledge, communication and so on. Remember you are not the sum total of your possessions.

The Law of Acceptance

Because truth is absolute acceptance of truth is absolute. Resisting such a reality will not succeed. In a practical way acceptance of things that we cannot change works to our advantage and makes our life easier to bear. For example: acceptance of the laws of the universe; acceptance of our birth circumstances; acceptance of blows that fate dishes out to us over which we have no control. Acceptance of the differences in others who differ from us, accepting to take responsibility for our thoughts and actions, acceptance of any situation as it is. Genuine acceptance of a situation is the first step towards finding the solution to turn things around for the better. This law does not mean you to sit back and to be passive to allow everything just to happen to you. On the contrary, it requires you to be fully aware, to be able to distinguish, to see things for what they are and to accept them. Acceptance of a situation as it is facilitates you taking action in the right direction.

The Law of Accommodation

Accommodation as a direct aspect of love is mandatory. According to this law failure to accommodate others and us is a violation of the law of Love and this violation sets into motion the universal law of Karma. Other words for accommodation are agreement, reconciliation, service, compromise, bargaining, settlement, trade off, concession, give and take, empathy and finding a middle ground. What this law, therefore, means is one should be open and willing to find a common ground to meet for any kind of dispute or disagreement. Try to see the other person's point of view, standpoint, and be open to negotiate. So if you act stubborn, fixed in your ideas, forcing your will on others refusing to settle, to finding a common ground beneficial to both, then you are not only going against the energies of this law but with your refusal you activate the law of Cause and Effect.

The Law of Action

We are each a focal point of energy and it is more desirable if we were a conscious focal point. No matter what we feel or know, no matter what our potential gifts or talents are, no matter what wonderful ideas we have, only our action can bring them to life. Those of us who think that we understand concepts such as commitment, courage and love discover one day that we actually only have this knowingness when we have acted and experienced these traits ourselves. It is only through doing ourselves and through experiencing that we are able to understand.

The Law of Action and Reaction

In the chaos that we live in today, as a focal point of energy we are expected individually to remember the law of economy of force and not to scatter our energies by reacting, resisting or repelling, emotionally to chaotic circumstances. Our effort should be more focused on keeping our emotions stable and steady and to use our common sense. In other words mind over lower emotions.

This does not mean that our lower emotions have to be denied, on the contrary, all our emotions need to be understood and digested. The lower emotions, however, such as anger, fear, envy, jealousy, insecurity, depression and doubt need to be guided by the mind. This will allow constructive forces from the Higher Self, such as love, courage, kindness, generosity, and from all those who work for order to pour through the lower self and to radiate out to the surroundings. To be able to do this we must learn to detach ourselves, to take distance and to discriminate by seeing the true sense of values. In this way we can be separated from the problem, and we can act instead of reacting blindly to circumstances. This will help us to keep our strength, it will allow time to be economized and the energies will be wisely distributed. We become constructive helpers contributing towards the solutions rather than being part of and losing ourselves deeper in the problems.

The Law of Activity

The law of Activity represents uninterrupted flow of activity. This law ascertains that with awareness, concentration and focus on a goal one can accomplish more with less strain.

The more blessing life bestows upon you, the more you are expected to give back to life. This is the way towards gaining illumination. The more you get from life the more you should take responsibility and to give back in kind service in order to keep the balance. Not only the Cosmos but also everyone around you will expect that from you.

The following might sound familiar to some of you: 'It's not fair, it seems that the more I do, the more everyone expects me to do!' Well this law explains why it is so and why it is fair after all. You are able to do more because you have more blessings, wealth, assets, gifts, talent, or energy that enable you to do more, therefore, you are expected to give back more in return. When you think about it and understand this law it does seem to make sense after all.

The Law of Adaptation

The law of Adaptation in time and space is the law of Economy or the line of least resistance. This line of least resistance is what is sought for and followed on the matter side of existence. Brahma manifests Will because he is Purpose and Love because in this solar system Love is the line of least resistance. Brahma is also Activity and Intelligence and his main characteristic is Adaptability. This law governs the rotary movement of any atom on every plane and sub plane. To interpret this law in plain words and to make it practical for us, this law represents metamorphosis, conversion, reformation, modification, transformation and major change. The line of least resistance means for us to have the ability to change and to adapt as the circumstances demand of us. There is a Chinese proverb that says that we should learn to be flexible like a tree that moves, sways and bends with the wind. If we are too inflexible and refuse to adjust to circumstances we would break as the tree would if it were standing too rigid and unyielding in a storm. In our solar system love is the line of least resistance. This means that if we can cultivate the feeling of love for life in general, we will have the strength to adapt easily whenever necessary.

The Law of Adjustment

This law is also known as the law of Balance. This law is elaboration and continuation of the law of Equalities. The law of Balance is a universal law that supersedes all of man's laws. Creating stability for all third dimension manifestation. Each thought must be balanced by whomever creates it. This is divine wisdom. This law requires us to allow room for all viewpoints without feeling that we must defend our own. Allow no one to tell you what your journey must reflect or what your reality is in life. Do not give your power away easily, but do give your love unconditionally. Any message communicated in love validates equality. Keep in mind that low self esteem is just as non-productive as a puffed up sense of self esteem for they both deny equality. Another manifestation of the imbalance of this law is all kinds of addiction. Any addiction to food, drugs, drink, tobacco, people, work, habit, idea or belief sets to work negative energies that go against this law.

When mind, body and spirit are totally in balance, harmony and peace is flowing and you know that you are applying more and more of the universal laws, there is a fair exchange. All things in nature in all its complexity are always in balance and connected in spite of the differences. This idea is clear enough and needs no elaborating on. See also the law of Attraction and Repulsion.

The Law of Affection

The law of Affection states that affection is a beam of love that may light upon a subject and create an object of adoration. Through this law we can hold someone close to us but at the same time have our arms wide open, wishing to see all creatures as free beings by freeing them from ourselves and from themselves, their fears, guilt inhibitions and from everything that hides their preciousness.

The law of Affection possesses not and yet sacrifices nothing of itself because it gives without expectation even from the joy in giving. As the sun must shine just to be the sun, so must affection be given if one is to be affectionate. The law of Affection cannot be manipulated or controlled, for its only purpose is to give. You cannot possess or use this law, but if you open your heart it enters and possesses your heart and uses it to shine its warmth of love upon the world. Make a conscious effort to include the feeling of affection for yourself and for others into your life and experience how miraculously your life becomes richer, fuller, bigger and better.

The Law of Affinity

The human organism is a microcosm which exactly reflects the macrocosm, the universe, this means that man and the universe are bound together by numerous correspondences. All of Esoteric Science is based on the law of Correspondences. There is an absolute correspondence between man and the universe. Each organ of man's body has a special affinity with a specific region of the universe. The organs of the cosmos and ours have something identical in common. Through the law of Affinity we make contact with the centers and worlds which correspond to certain elements within us. Knowledge of these correspondences opens a whole new world of possibilities for us.

This law is also known as the law of Sympathy or Resonance. Thanks to this universal law we can draw on the immense reservoirs of the universe to obtain all the elements we need as long as we project thoughts and feelings into space of the same sort as those that we want to attract to ourselves. It is the nature of our thoughts and feelings that determines which forces and elements we attract to ourselves. This law is the most important law for us to understand and is worth contemplating on because when we can really understand the workings of this law we will have a magic wand in our hands.

Everything in life is connected so you can actually set to work immediately to attract to yourself radiant particles forces of nature that you will begin to improve in every way. As you feel better and better every day you will radiate this around you to everyone you meet. When those who live and work with you see how happy you are and feel how radiant you are, you will seem more intelligent, stronger, and forceful, they will be drawn to you and they will have a better opinion of you. This in turn will make you feel even better about yourself and will change your destiny. Unfortunately, many of us are too busy complaining or are too busy being unhappy and then we blame everyone but ourselves for our misfortunes. We need to remember that we can determine our own destination by our own inclinations, tastes and desires.

The Law of Akasha

Akasha is a great cosmic law which is the principal of the intelligence of substance. The Akasha records of all life on earth are found on the etheric level available to see for all those who qualify. Those who qualify are evolved and trained initiates who are able to see the records on the psychic level, invisible for everyone else. Everything in life and everyone in every minute detail is recorded on the Akasha level.

Our planet consists of land and water and above that air. Above the air is 'ether'. Ether is the fifth cosmic element, subtle spiritual essence or a substance that pervades all space. Akasha is a Hindu word for ether. Ether is a subtler state of matter and it is on the etheric plane where all planets are connected on the level of their soul. Man and woman are considered miniature planets and both are more than just their physical bodies. Their beings, emanations and radiation reach out far into space and the action of their aura and magnetic field can be felt at great distances. The human being by means of the subtle bodies can reach out and unite with other souls and with the Soul of the Universe. This is how prayer and meditation work.

The artist, for example, who wants to create a masterpiece, cannot remain on the level of the five senses. The artist must rise to the higher etheric levels and unite her/himself with the Creator, to tap in to the sublime beauty of the Divine, in order to receive some divine particles, which the artist can then communicate in the work that is being created. See the law of Telepathy, the law of Creation, the law of Prayer and the law of Meditation.

The Law of the Alpha and Omega

All that is now was then and will be and has always been, so there is nothing new in the Universe. 'I am the Alpha and the Omega, the beginning and the end,' saith the Lord, 'which is and which was, and which is to come, the Almighty.' (Revelations 1:8.) We refer to the Alpha and Omega when we refer to the most important part of something.

Margo Kirtikar Ph.D.

The Law of Analogy

This law is also known as the law of Correspondence. The human organism infinitely small is a microcosm and an exact replica of the vast universe, the macrocosm. There are points and zones between man and the universe that correspond. All esoteric science is based on this law of Correspondence between the human and the universe. Each organ of the human body has an affinity with a given region of the cosmos. Since we humans have destroyed the original ideal relationship with the macrocosm and the Higher Powers, our task now is to restore this bond. This we are able to do because when we were created we were given all that we needed to evolve, to develop and in case we got lost, to find our way back home again. Every spirit that incarnates on this earth possesses all the spiritual faculties that correspond to all the virtues and qualities in the cosmos and so everything is possible. This obviously cannot be done all at once but gradually through learning, training, persistence, if the incarnated soul abides by the laws, the human evolves and eventually learns how to use these in-born faculties.

The law in question here works like this. If you have two identical tuning forks and you set one of them vibrating you will find that the other one vibrates too without you touching it. This is known as resonance. Vibrations are a means of communication. Exactly the same thing happens between the human being and the cosmos. If we attune our physical and our psychological being to the same vibrations as those of the universe, we can reach out, establish a bond and interact. We can even do more than that. We can further learn to set certain forces in motion and draw them to ourselves so that we can benefit from them through cultivating positive emotions such as: kindness, love, selflessness, goodwill and generosity. These are energies that will work with forces that automatically bring everything into harmony within you. You simply have to entertain elevated thoughts and feelings and they will set your spiritual centers vibrating harmoniously. No matter what religion we believe in, we are constantly told to love and honor one another, to be kind and generous, to exercise harmlessness and to be selfless. Well now you can understand why this is important. Namely, when we cultivate positive attributes in our character we align ourselves with the universal laws which in turn activates positive forces in our life.

The Law of Archetype

The Archetypal law is that law which is the prototype for the echoing reflections of other laws. The law of Archetype is that which serves as the skeleton or framework for other laws. The first Archetypal law is the law of One, The second is the law of Two, the third is the law of Three. This apparent division as never ending so long as the law of Description is in effect. Concepts and personalities, number, shapes, forms, situations that serve as patterns for others to follow are archetypes, even as the pyramid was an archetype for the hierarchy systems, and the zodiac shall be the archetype for the New World.

The Law of Ascension

This law defines the high vibration frequency of the soul at which an incarnated being is resonating. To reach this stage a personality loses the illusion of separation from its God self and becomes one.

One has gone through the process of purification. The vibration of such a person raises to the point of ascension. This also means that this soul need no longer to reincarnate and leaves the earth plane to live a finer existence on a higher plane. Jesus ascended as have many other Avatars before him and after him. We are meant to bring our loving energies to our every day existence, to set a good example and be a role model for others to emulate. We can recognize this higher vibration frequency in others by the degree to which such a person is a magnet to others. All Hierarchy and Heavenly Masters are ascended humans. Everyone of them has had to go through the process of life as a human on this earth. See also the law of Vibration.

The Law of Assembly

Through relinquishment one arrives to this law of Assembly. As the world makes progress through the law of Evolution there is a never ending process of elimination going on, accompanied by a parallel process of substitution. The old and purposeless is constantly abandoned for the new and the more useful. Throughout history, that which is no longer useful is rejected and discarded, and is replaced by more useful elements. We are presently for example, experiencing a process of re-interpreting and re-arranging what is known as doctrinal structure underlying the relation between knowledge and wisdom. This involves the destruction of old outdated concepts and institutions, substituting them with new and more correct ideas. Whether it is economics, politics, education or religion this process of ending and replacement continues. Old concepts must be discarded and new concepts have to be found. A new world religion for example will eventually be founded upon a deeper spiritual perception of life. In other words a spiritual unfoldment must consciously give way to a much higher phase of perception.

This law also works on an individual level for each one of us. It requires us to continually reevaluate our position in life and to discard the old and the useless structures, ideas and beliefs that no longer serve us effectively and to replace these with the new and more useful.

The Law of Attraction

This is the basic law of all manifestation, the Love Aspect, and it governs the Soul aspect. It is one of the three major laws, and it has eleven subsidiary laws. Fundamentally, this law describes the compelling force of attraction that holds our solar system to the Sirian. It holds our planets revolving around our central unit, the sun. It holds the lesser systems of atomic and molecular matter circulating around a center in the planet, and that of the subtle bodies coordinated around their microcosmic center. It is the primary law of man.

The quality that emerges through the process of manifestation and under the impulse of divine life, is love. Love functions through the medium of the law of Attraction. Love has one sole aim and that is to produce an ultimate synthesis in consciousness. The object of the present evolutionary process is the growth of conscious awareness and the entire process is directed towards that. Both love and sex express the meaning of the law of Attraction. Love is sex and sex is love, for in those two words the relation, the interplay and the union between God and His universe, between the human and God, between human and her/his own soul and between men and women are equally depicted. We refer here to sex with higher emotions of love and respect for life and not to the physical animal act that satisfies the lower physical senses. The law of Attraction determines the present and governs the immediate condition of the planetary types. It is concerned with the soul or the consciousness aspect.

Margo Kirtikar Ph.D.

The Law of Attraction and Repulsion

This is one of the three major Cosmic laws. The law of Attraction is neutral because it is also called the law of Adjustment. This law is the fire which is produced by the merging during evolution of the two poles, the negative and the positive. It is the law of Akasha. Fundamentally, this law describes the compelling force of attraction that holds our solar system to the Sirian. It holds our planets revolving around our central unit, the sun. It holds the lesser systems of atomic and molecular matter circulating around a center in the planet, and that of the subtle bodies coordinated round their microcosmic center. This is the basic law of all manifestation, the love aspect and it governs the Soul aspect. And it has eleven subsidiary laws. It is the primary law of man. The law of synthesis is beginning to be felt. Like attracts like. We attract people of like energy. This means if you want to attract different friends, mates, circumstances etc. then you must change yourself within. If you are a negative thinking person, you will attract negative people. If you are co-dependent person, you will attract controlling people. You must first take control of your thoughts and that will change your life and your manifestations. If you change yourself to being a positive thinker, or a non-co-dependent person you will become a healthier person in every way.

The law of attraction can be stated this way: As you seek, you attract and are attracted to that which will fulfill your search. This law applies only when you seek. You attract to yourself that which you put the energy of your thoughts into. If you desire something, you can attract it to you by positively anticipating its arrival into your life. Alternately, you can attract that which you do not want into your life by giving negative energy to your thoughts of receiving it. In practical words, as an example, if you constantly think while driving, I'm afraid I'll have an accident or I don't want to have an accident, then you are sure to attract an accident.

The underlying law that regulates supply in the world of effects has two important phases, one is desire and the other expectation. These mental attitudes represent lines of attractive forces, the former being the positive phase of the law and the latter the negative phase, while phases must be complied with to obtain the best and greatest results.

The first phase of desire embraces a positive process of attraction; that is, when an individual earnestly desires a thing he sets up a line of force that connects him with the invisible side of the good that is desired. Should he weaken or change in his desire that particular line of force is disconnected or misses its goal. If, however, he remains constant in his desire or ambition the good remains constant in his desire and sooner or later it will be realized. The principle involved is that you cannot ask for anything unless it already exists, if not in form, then in substance; and desire is the motive power for calling it forth to manifest into visible appearance or physical effect.

It is no use to desire a thing unless you expect to get it, either in part or in full. Desire without expectation is idle wishing or dreaming. You simply waste much valuable mental energy in doing this. Desire will put you in touch with the inner world of causes and connect you by invisible means with the substance of the thing desired; then, continuous expectation is necessary to bring it into a reality in your life. Much like the pull of gravitation in the physical realm, 'expectation' is a drawing force of the mind which acts in the invisible realm.

Often people desire good things which they never expect nor make any real effort to grasp. They start out well and may get halfway, but not any further. When they learn to comply with the other half of the process involved and learn to expect what they desire, most of their dreams or wishes will steadily materialize. We meet people who expect things they do not want but which often come. This proves that expectation is a powerful attractive force. Never expect a thing you do not want, and never desire a thing you do not expect. When you expect something you do not want, you attract the undesirable, and when you desire a thing that is not expected, you simply disintegrate valuable mental force. On the other hand, when you constantly expect that which you persistently desire, your ability to attract becomes irresistible. Desire connects you with the thing desired and expectation draws it into your life.

When we charge our thoughts so firmly with the idea that there are no failures, then we expect success. Our mind becomes strengthened with our conviction and, like a magnet, draws to us whatever desire is uppermost at the time. One attracts into ones life ones deepest desire. We do not get what we deserve, we get what we believe we deserve.

The Law of Authority

This law states that whoever is liable has the authority, and to the degree of that liability the degree of authority should be given. The author of an action or work who is liable for that work has the authority over that work, to dispose of as he or she wishes, along with the liability. The Creator has absolute authority over all creation.

The Law of Averages

The law of Averages is the principle holding that probability will influence all occurrences in the long term.

The Law of Awareness

For most people, awareness depends on their senses and each one is attracted to different things. When the soul is aware of itself and one is aware of one's soul, then the senses follow that which has awareness of the whole. All that one loves with the senses is temporary as one's body imperishable. Only the soul and God are infinite and eternal. The realization of this is a far greater gift than what one can possess here on earth. Material possessions cannot be taken when the soul has departed from the body. The soul, however, departs with the intangible refined qualities that may have been acquired during a life time.

This law is about us observing our thoughts, feelings, behavior and actions, to be aware of the illusion and the separateness we experience and yet not to be confused by this illusion and not to be caught in it. To be aware of the illusion of tragedy, free will or death and not to be caught in it and to realize it is nothing but illusion. There are certain limitations placed upon this awareness which the law cannot break. One of these is that it cannot break its own principles and laws. It cannot deny or reject those who would appear to separate themselves from this awareness. Having awareness is having the ability to distinguish and not to believe everything that one reads, sees or hears but always to question, to explore and to discover, to have soul awareness.

The Law of Balance

This is elaboration and continuation of the law of Equalities or Fair Exchange. The law of Balance is a universal law that supersedes all of man's laws, creating stability for all third dimension manifestation. Each thought must be balanced by whomever creates it. This is divine wisdom. For every action there is a reaction. The energy of the universe is continuously flowing from action to reaction in search of balance to achieve harmony. Where there is an imbalance we usually experience irritation, discomfort and pain.

Duality of perception leads to perfect balance that governs the universal law of One. Negative and positive create a perfect balance and do not negate the law of One. Any message communicated in love validates equality. Low self-esteem is just as non productive as a puffed up sense of self esteem. They both deny equality. Another manifestation of the imbalance of this law is addiction. See also the law of Adjustment and the law of Attraction and Repulsion.

The law of Cosmic Balance is considered to be the foundation for the universe wherein the forces of nature are in a state of constant equilibrium. However, the equilibrium of the universe is not absolute because there is a constant oscillation and it is this slight lack of equilibrium that keeps the universe in constant motion perpetually active. If there was a perfect balance and harmony the universe would be in a state of inertia, stagnant, absolutely immobile and manifestation would not be possible. The vital thing is that this imbalance should not be too great or else it would lead to total destruction. The key is to learn to work with the forces and not to sway too far from that golden middle line. In other words avoid extremes.

Margo Kirtikar Ph.D.

The Law of Being

The base of the spine is controlled and governed by the law of Being where Spirit and matter meet. We are told that the 'life principle' is seated in the heart and the 'will to be' is seated in the base of the spine and from the angle of the esoteric sciences houses a threefold thread. This threefold thread within the spinal column is therefore, composed of three threads of energy which have channeled for themselves in the substance of the interior of the column a 'threefold way of approach and of withdrawal.' These are called in the Hindu terminology: the 'ida,' the 'pingala' and the 'sushumna' paths and they together form the path of life for the individual human. One of these paths is the one along which the energy which feeds matter is poured. Another is related to the path of consciousness and of sensitive psychic unfoldment. The third is the path of pure spirit. At the base of the spine lies dormant the serpent of fire known as the 'kundalini fire.' Under normal circumstances this fire is aroused when the human has evolved to a certain degree of consciousness. It is popular in the west to have workshops specifically to arouse this kundalini fire prematurely. This can be at times extremely dangerous mentally for the individual because normally the kundalini fire when aroused naturally requires the person to have achieved a certain state of consciousness on the evolution ladder and for the body to have arrived to a certain vibratory level. When the kundalini fire is aroused or forced before the person has developed his physical instruments and spiritual faculties, the kundalini fire which rises through the nerves of the spine to the brain can cause irreparable mental damage and mental disorientation. Read also the law of Meditation.

The Law of Believing and Knowing

We can create, and it is through believing and knowing we will manifest our desires. It is critical though that the believing comes from the emotional heart, and most importantly, allowing this to happen. The knowing here does not refer to book knowledge but the knowing beyond any doubt with every cell and fiber of one's being.

The Law of Challenge

We have the right to ask another of his or her intent and whatever pertinent information we feel we require when encountering a disembodied being. Those who come to us in the role of information givers to channeling mediums, do not mind being challenged. Ask the entity your questions three times using the same words each time and you will be given the correct information.

Margo Kirtikar Ph.D.

The Law of Change

In the ancient formulations of the Archives of the Hierarchy it is stated: 'Regard and recognize the changes in the hearts of men and change the rules as men in time and cyclic change approach the Ashram. The Ashram stands not still. New Life pours in from either side.' From this we learn that the law of Change governs the hierarchy just as it governs humanity. The occult law holds good, 'As above so below.' What we also learn from this statement is that the disciple who functions under this law has to deal with (a) constant transformation in the personality and to adapt the self rapidly to developing and changing events which are taking place and (b) to contribute to the wise circulation and direction of the new energies which are pouring into and through the Ashram. This is done by realizing that one is the center of changing energies. The new energies pouring through Shamballa into the Hierarchy are of an extra planetary nature and have their source largely in the 'Aquarian' quality of the present cycle and these energies are steadily eliminating the energies of the 'Piscean' age.

On a more practical note for us this law says that everything is constantly in a state of change and constantly growing and transforming to something better and higher. Change occurring in the physical structure, in the personality, in consciousness and in the changing of events individually and collectively. This law does not tolerate stagnation on any level. We humanity are presently witnessing a period of extreme change and adjustment and of a far reaching organization. Evolutionary changes instinctively demand major reorganization and group recognition, great work and responsibility. The three lines of thought for us to urgently meditate on presently in our time are progressive change, reordering change and above all group responsibility on every level, social, economical, political and educational.

In accordance with this law of Transmutation every condition can be transmuted and everything is always changing. The only consistent thing in the Universe is the imperishability of energy and its changing form. This law is also known as the law of Alchemy which allows every condition in life to be transmuted into divine glory and made spiritually beautiful no matter what that condition is. If we can accept a situation, no matter how bad it is, bless it and are thankful to God, we can actually transmute even bitter heart breaking experiences into spiritual godliness. Through this law we can receive the power also to transmute our spiritual dreams to physical manifestation. This alchemy is the power of God in action and is eternal and immutable.

The Law of Chemical Affinity

This law governs the soul aspect of the mineral kingdom. It concerns the marriage of the atoms, and the romance of the elements. It serves to continue the life of the mineral kingdom and to preserve its integrity.

The Law of Co-creation

The law of Co-Creation states that two people working in co-creative action have the power of four people working individually, and three working in co-creative activity have the power of nine people working individually. Four working in co-creative activity have the power of sixteen and one hundred and forty-four persons working in harmony can change the world.

When large groups of beings believe and agree on certain images as real and being stable, this agreement holds the power of many times that number of energies, if such energies were held by individuals working separately. Wherein groups agree upon certain images, these images do tend to manifest and hold their being in a magnified manner. Jesus said: 'All these things ye shall do also.' We human are co-creators with the Higher Powers but a human being must reach a certain height in the evolution ladder in order to have the power be able to create.

The Law of Choice

This law states that we humans are given the freedom to choose whatever it is we desire to do or not do, for better or for worse, and no one should influence us or rob us of that choice. Throughout history individuals have exercised power over others and have, therefore, consistently violated this law. See the law of Free Will.

The Law of Circulation/Circle

Experiences in life both the positive and the negative are nothing but lessons presented to us individually and collectively in the school of life. Each time a lesson is presented to you, and you do not learn from this particular lesson, or you avoid the lesson, it will be repeated with more energy, presenting you with another opportunity to learn. This is repeated again and again until you have learned the lesson. If you think that by ignoring or postponing an unpleasant situation that it will disappear forever or at best take care of itself eventually, you are mistaken. The problem will confront you again challenging you to remember and to act, in order for you to learn your lesson from the school of life.

Everything in life goes round in a circle. This also means that whatever energy you send out, whatever the quality, will ultimately go round the circle and in time find its way back to you. This law also states that which is in circulation increases and that which is hoarded decreases. A classical example of this is the circulation of money and economics. In the eastern tradition of Feng Shui, the studies of energy, we speak of stagnating energy which blocks the general flow of energy. In other words if we wish to have something or someone new in our life, we have to first move, rearrange and clear out old things or issues in order to allow space for the new. The closing of a circle also means the completion of something. The law does not allow loose ends.

The Law of Coalescence

On the path of involution this law controls the primal gathering together of molecular matter, beneath the atomic sub plane. It is the basis of the attractive quality that sets in motion the molecules and draws them into the needed aggregations. It is the measure of the sub planes. The atomic sub plane sets the rate of vibration. The law of Cohesion fixes the coloring of each plane. See also the law of Cohesion.

The Law of Cohesion

This law is one of the seven laws of the Solar System under the three major laws and is also referred to as the law of Birth. It is a branch of the law of Attraction. It is the first molecular plane of the system and is the home of the Monad. Divine coherency is demonstrated. This law states that it is the aim of all things to unite. Unification, is a simultaneous attraction between two or more, as in sex, business partners and organization, political groups and so on. See also the law of Coalescence.

The Law of Color

All colors emanate from one primary color, one source, the cosmic ray of indigo, veiling cosmic love and wisdom. This indigo color splits into three major colors and then into the four minor, making the seven colors of the spectrum. It is written that colors as they manifest on the physical level as seen by the physical eye are at their crudest and hardest in comparison as they appear on the emotional plane and become even finer and more beautiful on other planes of existence. Many have through meditation and receptiveness to higher teaching gone through the Hall of Learning to the Hall of Wisdom that is where the true esoteric interpretation of the colors can be known. Meditation prepares one for the initiation that opens the door to the Hall of Wisdom.

This law states that color serves a twofold purpose. It acts as a veil for something that lies behind and is therefore attracted to the central spark. All colors are centers of attraction and are complimentary or are antipathetic to each other. Color like music can be healing and impacts the physical, emotional, mental and human body profoundly. Man is also partially composed of color in the aura. We are color, tone symbols and speed of vibration and light. When intense rays of one or more colors are sent to a specific area of the body, the result is change in our psyche and structure.

We in the west, are beginning to rediscover the importance that color plays in our environment and the effects that colors have on our health. With color therapy we are able to heal illnesses, of a psychic nature, since the physical is dependent on the psyche. We can direct our emotional and mental health by surrounding ourselves with harmonic rainbow and bright colors. Just the same as we can do with essence and smell of various natural herbs and flowers. Crystals most of which also come in colors are another source of healing. In nature which itself gives us a magnificent combination and variety of colors there exists all that we need to heal ourselves.

The Law of Common Ground

This law is viewed as a problem solving approach and is an area where two or more people can gather to blend their differences. The law requires that the area be cleansed of previous energy left by others who historically have passed through, or have lived on the spot. This is done by two or more people sending loving energy to the area for a specified period of time. After the cleansing process one surrounds the area with a gold net to keep it cleansed and protected from other negative energies. The energy left after using the space for the blending of differences can be cleansed in the same manner. All this is done on a psychic level through the power of the higher mind and imagination.

The Law of Communication

Spirit communicates with itself. Language does not exist, except as a physical manifestation. Therefore communication is a divine aspect of God, and excludes no soul. All that may be known truly is known depending on the level of growth of each soul. The higher evolved the soul is, the more clear is the communication with the spirit. Evolved souls are able to communicate with each other without words and through telepathy over great distances. On a practical level no harmonious inter relationship can exist without clear communication. It is the duty of the more educated, the more evolved or the wiser to make that extra effort to establish better communication with fellow humans.

The Law of Compassion

Compassion for another Soul is compassion for Spirit. Judgement, which excludes compassion, is without merit. Failure to show compassion is a violation of the Universal law of Love and sets into motion the Universal law of Karma. One has to feel compassion first before one can feel the energy of love. Having compassion does not mean feeling pity, but rather it is the feeling with someone of pain and suffering as if it were our own. Having empathy with rather than feeling sympathy with. Compassion is free of judgement and of criticism.

The Law of Compensation

The law of Compensation is closely related to the law of Sacrifice. For this law to become active in your life and to become a recognized factor in daily living sacrifice is required. Sacrifice has nothing to do with animal or blood offerings. The compensation comes later into recognition. The rewards of a happy and fruitful life are attainable if you understand the terms of this law. The abundant supply of all we need is ever attainable and at hand, if we take responsibility to change our application of natural law in order to bring about the conditions that we aspire for. If you think you do not deserve compensation you will not get it. The law follows your belief. If you think you are unjustly treated by life and others are getting more than you are, then perhaps you should look at yourself again and ask yourself whether you have really paid your dues. Paying your dues is a popular term we use. In other words you must have had done some work, sacrificed something, given of yourself in some way in order to get the compensation in return. This law sees to it that we all get what we are owed. What you invest in life is the return you receive. What effort and energy you place in your actions of giving, plays a big role in what your return will be. The main aspect of this law is balance, which regulates what is returned to us for our efforts. When we apply honor, integrity, and purity in our efforts and action of thought we initiate a purity of compensative response. We have heard it said, 'what comes around goes around,' this gesture holds true, for if we cheat, deceive and lie through our efforts we receive nothing in compensation but grief. We must work within the parameters of natural law, and when we work diligently and consistently we find our efforts are rewarded, the foundation and walls of our house of success are strong and coinciding with the workings of natural forces. Compensation is an equal return for that which is given. It is a balance of that quality or service that is extended to another. In order to receive anything worth while in life we must first give. Often we think that we are working hard or contributing and doing our share, but in reality we are being short sighted and selfish concentrating on our own self centered needs and satisfactions. Our striving and our achievements should be in accordance with our gifts, abilities and talents, which we should endeavor to put to work for the good of the whole. The more we give, the more we do, the more we contribute, with unselfish genuine motives the more we will be compensated and the compensation might bot always be that what we imagined it to be.

The Law of Completion

On a cosmic level, at the point of omega all souls transmute to become the energy vibration of God at which point the Group Soul begins as Alpha. In practical terms we could interpret this law for us on the physical level, as one that requires us to bring everything to a close, be this a project or a relationship. Unfinished business, open loose ends are not tolerated by nature. If we really give this a further thought, we ourselves are very aware of this as we feel when something in our lives remains incomplete. We have this inner gnawing feeling that haunts us and will not let loose until we attend to it one way or another.

The Law of Concentration

The focus of the soul strengthens thought and brings thought into physical manifestation. Distraction, which is a function of the lower mind, is a tool of the soul created in order to develop concentration and thus aids in manifestation. See the Universal law of Balance. One needs to cultivate the concentration power in order to create and manifest into the material world. Without total focus and concentration nothing can be properly achieved. Concentration power is a quality of the soul.

The Law of Condensing Light

This law is for those who are ready to create profound changes in their consciousness, in their spiritual path and in their daily life. Working with the solar light, is one of the most powerful forces in the universe. It is a light of higher will and universal love. It is the light of the soul plane.

The essence of your purpose on earth is to work with the Solar Light to fulfill the essence of your soul's higher purpose that is to become a more perfect light. To find light, to draw light into yourself, and to become the light as your radiance lights the way for others. In the process of working with Solar Light, you are guided to meet the Solar Light and draw it into your mind, emotions, body, aura, atoms, and every part of your life. You will learn how to bring Solar Light and its qualities of radiance into your circumstances, projects, relationships, and activities to enhance all the light that is there, and to release anything that is not light.

You discover how to recognize who and what increases your light, and how to work with those things that decrease your light. Your vision of what is possible in your life can expand and you will know what steps to take to create what you want. You learn how to manifest those forms that hold the most light for you. You learn how to create matter and form out of light. You learn to manifest those things that increase your light and that are in harmony with your higher purpose.

You link your mind with the Universal Mind to know what actions to take to bring about what you want. You work with and become aware of the Solar Light from moment to moment.

Margo Kirtikar Ph.D.

As you become aware of both the higher dimensions of light and your ordinary reality simultaneously, you can consistently see and choose your path of most light in everything you do, making those choices in every moment that assist you in becoming a more perfect light. All this is possible for us to do through focus, vision, concentration, meditation and prayer. Focus on the solar light and flood it through any form or situation to cleanse, purify and protect.

The Law of Consciousness

The development of the human being is but the passing from one state of consciousness to another in a succession of expansions and a growth in awareness. Consciousness is dependent upon the physical body for expression and both are dependent upon life and energy for existence. It is the expansion of consciousness and increase in sensitivity and awareness that is the goal of all divine and hierarchical effort.

Consciousness is equal to soul. Soul consciousness. The more we are in contact and in union with the individual soul the more the soul can manifest itself through the personality on this earth. As consciousness expands, the space for events increases and therefore, the dimension which one recognizes good and evil, opportunities and possibilities, past present future enlarge to reveal the outstanding needs in this present world cycle. There is individual consciousness, group consciousness, nation consciousness, global consciousness and universal consciousness. Spirit is pure consciousness and pure thought. Nothing exists outside of thought. Consciousness of God. Everything in the universe has its origin in idea, in thought and it has its completion in the manifestation of thought through form. Soul is the thinker of thoughts. The consciousness responds when directed by soul, which is beyond all thought, beyond all matter, energy, space and time. As we change in our state of consciousness our physical body responds to this change, and everything around us begins to change for us, including our likes and dislikes. Even our nutritional diet changes according to our state of consciousness.

We each are born with a certain amount of consciousness but from then until our death, we are responsible to make the effort to reach higher and beyond, to reach greater states of consciousness.

When you hold your consciousness firmly upon something, you bring exactly that into existence in yourself. It is impossible for your life to contain anything other than that which is your present or past accumulation of consciousness. Whatever it is that you are conscious of, in thought and feeling, stamps itself upon the Universal substance in and around you and brings it ultimately forth into your life.

The goal is to be constantly aware of what you are thinking about, to be aware of your surroundings, the environment, to be aware of the company you keep, of your every activity, what you read and what you expose yourself to. All of these things leave a stamp on your consciousness and on the universal consciousness that in turn manifests this again in your life. When a man is group conscious, he is aware of his soul group, of the soul in all forms and has attained a stage of Christlike perfection as the 'Measure of the stature of the fullness of the Christ' (Eph.IV:13). See the law of Thought, the law of Rebirth and the law of the Soul.

The Law of Continuity of Consciousness

The universe is in a continuous and endless process of creation. Cosmic consciousness is a reality and everything in creation is connected to everything else. The medium for the 'implicate order' of this relationship is consciousness. The fusion of individual consciousness and the universal consciousness which is known in occult language as the building of the 'antahkarana bridge' results in the development of universal knowledge, of omniscience, all science and all knowledge. Continuity of consciousness is achieved after the Soul has been acknowledged, awakened, liberated and identified with the Whole. This is known as 'enlightenment.' A step nearer to achieving enlightenment is to be aware of our thoughts, emotions and actions, a faculty that enables us to be vigilant, observant and knowing. Destruction of God's creation is not possible. Continuity is absolute. See the law of Soul.

The Law of Correlation

For every manifestation of spirit in the physical reality the corresponding thought first appears in spirit. 'As above so below.'

Nothing can manifest on earth if it does not exist in the spiritual world.

The Law of Cosmic Equation

The tables of law hidden in the Arc of the Covenant are the Logos, the word of reason, measure, relationship and number. In Genesis The Lord God said: "I have made everything with number, measure and weight." This law is also known as the law of Cosmic Equation. To possess the tables, is to have the possibility of access to the great 'Law of Unity' that rules the worlds, of relating effects with their causes and consequently, of acting on the phenomena that the causes produce as they diversify into plurality. However, man is still unable to make use of this information unless he has been initiated into the secret of reading them. The secret was sealed in a cryptic writing in a numerical system, which was given in the Semitic language by Moses, now known as the 'Kabbala.'

All numbers, measures and geometric forms have a meaning and only those who are initiated are able to understand this. The one who understands this understands the Universe. See also the law of Number, Measure and Weight.

The Law of Cosmic Manifestation

Every human desire defies the Cosmic law of the constructive use of energy. It is said that under every human desire lies a serpent coiled that will demand payment as sure as you are born. Just as sure as you exist in this Universe will you find every human desire coming back to you one day, demanding a price in pain, limitation and unhappiness for no other reason in the universe except that those desires defy the law of Cosmic Manifestation. This reminds us of the Buddhist teaching namely to be free of all desire. Some contemplation is required here to understand this correctly. See also the law of Desire.

The Law of Courage

The law of Courage states that courage is the ability to not only face a danger but to risk an action to defuse that danger. When action is taken fear departs. The degree of courage is in proportion to the degree of danger, risk and fear a courageous action must defuse. Courage is a quality of an evolved soul in manifestation. The more evolved the soul is the more courage the person has and the less fear one feels.

Courage is a soul quality.

Margo Kirtikar Ph.D.

The Law of Creativity

There are physical laws like gravity and relativity that govern our physical world and there are laws that govern our mental world. Just as there is law and order, structure and form in all existence there is law and order in the realm of creativity as well. People who accomplish their ideals are cooperating with the universal laws of nature. When we know and understand universal laws and cooperate with them we will be able to expend less energy and direct it more efficiently enabling us to create always higher and greater achievements. Through the practice of daily mental and spiritual discipline we are able to develop greater awareness of the universal laws. The Creator is absolutely creative and as extensions of the Creator we are creative and we are co-creators with God. Nothing exists for us in our individual and collective world, which we did not create ourselves. As soon as we formulate a desire in our heart it becomes a reality on a subtler level. We are responsible for all of our creations. Every human being has this deep instinct within him to seek and to create something better.

The power of imagination is essential for creativity. Everybody dreams, wishes and imagines but one needs to understand how this works in order to be creative. The imagination can be described as a screen that lies between the visible and the invisible worlds, and images and entities are projected on this screen that we are normally unaware of in our field of consciousness. Those who have a developed imagination are able to use this faculty of imagination, to receive and to record these impressions, which they then try to express or describe or realize on the physical plane. When one knows how to model and govern his own thoughts and feelings, he is capable of purifying his psyche to such an extent that his imagination becomes transparent and crystal clear and he begins to 'see' with his third eye the things on the subtler plane. At this level imagination and vision are one. The power of imagination is formative but it is the thought that creates. If the imagination is allowed to roam randomly, if it is not guided to some useful task by an intelligent will, it remains fruitless. Thousands all over the globe might have the same great idea all at the same time, but it is only the one who knows how to control and discipline the imagination who is able to manifest the idea on the material plane. See also the law of Abstraction.

The Law of Credibility

This law states that credibility is the ability of entities to earn, receive and accept credit for what they do, and to refuse credit for anything they have not done. Your credibility is the standard by which others may evaluate you to determine how they will relate to you.

The Law of Cycles

The world of nature exists within a larger pattern of cycles, such as day and night and the passing of the seasons. The seasons do not push one another, neither do clouds race the wind across the sky or vice versa. All things happen in good time and in their own time. Everything has a time to rise, and a time to fall. Whatever rises falls and whatever falls eventually rises again. That is the principle of cycles. This law is active everywhere, in everything and in all of us, in circumstances and events. History proves this. There are smaller cycles and there are larger cycles. With observation we can see and understand this law of cycles working in our own lives. All of life exists in cycles. For everything there is a beginning, an existence, and an end. To every thing there is a season, and a time to every purpose under the heaven. Through observing our own life closely and understanding the cycles of the highs and the lows, which can be three, seven or nine years cycles, we can figure out the rhythm of the cycles in our lives for outer activity, for intake and re-energizing and for rest and contemplation. This would help us to do the right thing at the right time as we go with the energy flow and have it work for us so we can be meet with success in our endeavors.

Margo Kirtikar Ph.D.

The Law of Cyclic Returns

Also known as The Wheel of Reincarnation. Reincarnation is that process by which the 'consciousness of the permanent atom' manifests in another body through the human birthing process. This accounts for genius in the very young. Once a soul qualifies for an incarnation to the third dimension, there is an understanding that it must be completed. All karma must be cleared or forgiven and certain aspects of soul growth accomplished before the entire cycle of reincarnation growth is considered completed.

Disintegration and death for all periods of transition are periods of the destruction and building of forms and the shattering of the old so that that the newer and better chalices of life may be constructed. This law governs the gradual disintegration of the concrete forms and their sacrifice to the evolving life. In a way this is the reverse side of the law of Vibration, it is the law that governs the end of a system. The law of Sacrifice and Death is the controlling factor of this aspect on the physical plane. The destruction of the form in order that the evolving life may progress is one of the fundamental methods in evolution. True death, under the law, is brought about by the attainment of the objective and hence by the cessation of aspiration. The etheric double of a human, a planetary Logos and a Solar Logos, being shattered, becomes non-polarized as regards its indweller and permits therefore an escape. It is no longer a source of attraction, nor a focal magnetic point. It becomes non-magnetic and the great law of Attraction ceases to control it, and so the form disintegrates.

The result is freedom from the handicaps of the physical vehicle allowing entrance into a fuller life. See also the law of Sacrifice and Death, the law of Reincarnation, the law of the Soul, the law of Vibration and the law of Attraction.

The Law of Description

The law of Description is a law that serves as a tool for creative purposes. This as likened unto the paint brush of the artist, the chisel of the sculptor. Description as that which carves out images, creates boundaries, creates shapes and forms, creates limitations, creates confinements, and creates also those concepts that expand those boundaries to release from confinement. The law of Description is capable of creating anything for anyone. This relates unto the law of Magic in that anything described is on its course toward creating a manifestation to the decree of impact on its description. The nature of manifestation depends upon the intensity of the collective or disruptive energies involved. In practice this means when we desire to manifest anything we need to visualize and imagine the picture in its totality with every minute detail and focus our concentration on this fixed image unchanged for it to materialize on the physical plane.

The Law of Desire

What one desires, he wills to be. What one wills to oneself, one first desired. To achieve one's goals in life, one must desire them. 'Ask, and it shall be given you.' 'Seek and ye shall find.' 'Knock, and it shall be opened unto you.' You need to take the initiative first but whatever it is that you desire should be for the good of all concerned, free of all selfish motives. Refer also to the law of Cosmic Manifestation.

The Law of Destiny

This law does not really apply to us, not at the present time anyway. This law affects the Ashram and the Hierarchy as a whole. This law of destiny has been brought into being since the foundation of the Hierarchy on earth. It is the result of the pledged and united dedication to service that is the outstanding note of the united Ashrams. It is a sevenfold law, for it takes on the seven color of the seven rays, the seven qualifications, modes, methods and energy expressions of all the seven rays. As far as humanity is concerned it is free from all evil because it is selflessly motivated. This law will become effective when humanity achieves increased purity in the three worlds.

Through the universal law of Planning, the blueprint for each soul, once created by the Higher Intelligence, cannot be subverted. Contrary to all beliefs we do not create our future but we do choose which direction our life should take. It is we who set our course but our destination is already there waiting for us. There are thousands of different regions and spheres in space and our path can lead us upwards or downwards all we have to do is make our choice.

The Law of Dharma

This law represents the Purpose of Life. The law of Dharma is that which may be described as the principle of 'Right Action'; this refers to that which is universally right, right for all who are affected by the action. An action by an individual, a group, a nation or culture is right only when everyone is rightly served by the action according to their needs and earnings. Dharma brings about that which may be called 'good karma' or 'right results'. Each living thing has a purpose for existence and a special experience to provide to this world. Utilizing our unique talents in service of others exalts our spirits to attain our ultimate goals.

To live a life without creating further karma is to do everything in the name of God or in the name of that Inner Master within you, to live in flow with the universal laws.

The Law of Differentiation

Also known as the law of Discernment. This law allows us to tap into our own unique piece of the Divine Blueprint. It is about being totally in tune with the next step in our personal evolution path and we are connected without judgment of other realities. It is about the recognition that there are many instruments in the 'Divine Orchestra' and knowing your place within this orchestra and what instrument you are to play and learning how to play harmoniously together with all the other instruments. We have learned through our many embodiments that the more finely we tune the physical vehicle, the stronger it is and the higher the voltage, frequency or light quota, we can attract and emit.

The sound which was the first indication of the activity of the planetyra Logos is not a word but a full reverberating sound holding within itelf all other sounds all chords and certain musical tones which have been given the name 'Music of the Spheres.' It is this sound that the rising one must recognize and respond to. This can be achieved by the student at the fourth initiation once he has let go of the ego. From the silence which is the sound the reverberating note of Shamballa the sounds focuses itself depending on the status of the initiate. At this stage the initiate is confronted with the seven paths, because each path constitutes a mode of penetrating into a realm of realization beyond our planet. The initiate must demonstrate his mastery of the law of Differentiation and arrive at a knowledge of the seven paths through differentiating the seven sounds, which make up the one sound, but which are not related to the seven sounds which compose the threefold AUM.

Being a 'refined human being' tuned to the beat of Oneness brings rewards of joy, magic, bliss, fulfillment, great soul to soul relationships, health, vitality and much more. We move from surviving to thriving, we activate four fifths of the brain housing higher consciousness, and we are conscious to the Divine Plan as we witness it unfold with great joy.

The Law of Discipline

Many problems can be avoided through exercising self discipline a quality one can cultivate. Discipline on an inner level has to do with self knowledge, knowing yourself, your strengths and limitations, it is recognizing your potential and how you can go beyond your limits.

Discipline is the surest means to greater freedom and independence. By practicing discipline, one expands to a greater degree than almost any other action. It provides the focus to achieve the skill level and depth of knowledge that translates into more options in life.

Commitment involves discipline over a specific period of time. Discipline and commitment provide the bridge between here and our goals. Nothing can be achieved without practicing discipline.

The Law of Disintegration

This is one of the seven laws of the Solar System. On the third plane comes the final casting off, the ultimate shedding of the sheaths, of the fivefold superman. A Chohan of the sixth Initiation discards all the sheaths beneath the monadic vehicle, from the atmic to the physical. It is the reverse aspect of the law of Cohesion. The law of Economy holds the key to this law. When the Monad has circled through all disintegrating forms and has achieved the sixth initiation, the five lesser sheaths are destroyed. This law governs the physical plane catastrophes and disruptions, the astral and the lower mental thoughts plane disintegration. This law breaks up the forms and the law of Attraction builds up the forms again.

We experience the break up of the forms of political control, great religious thought forms, art and science etc. All eventually break under the working of this law. The process is slow. A form comes into being and grows into a perfect form and at the moment it has reached perfection loses its usefulness, it crystallizes and breaks and the evolving life escapes to find itself new forms of greater adequacy. This is the case for all life as we know it and through all cosmic processes.

We go through the process of life, birth, growing, changing and expanding in consciousness, getting old and disintegrating and dying so that the soul can move on to another more adequate form to continue with the growth of consciousness and going through initiations. Nothing is static in the universe everything must move on constantly growing, changing reaching its full potential and finally disintegrating releasing the spirit within.

The Law of Dissolution

Disease and death are essentially conditions inherent in substance, just as long as a woman or man identifies her or himself with the form aspect, so will she or he be conditioned by the law of Dissolution. This law is a fundamental and natural law governing the life of the form in all the kingdoms of nature.

When the disciple or the initiate is identifying herself with the Soul and when the antakharana, the rainbow bridge, is built by means of the life principle at the demand of the Spiritual Will or through recognition of the necessities of the Hierarchy or the purposes of Shamballa, natural law uses or discards the body at will.

The Law of Divine Flow

We live in the law of Divine Flow by living in the moment, by being centered and by being in service to others, as opposed to service to the self. We stay in the moment by moment flowing of our higher self, creating actions that reflect love and allowingness.

When we are able to do this, we notice how we say just the right things, do what is best for all, and refrain from doing that which we previously disliked in ourselves or in others. Through the energies of this law we maintain a stronger connection to our Godself. The more we do this, the more we are able to go on doing this. To a degree, the deliberate letting go of this flow is the allowing of our spiritual integrity to be compromised.

The Law of Divine Union

Divine union does not require two or more people in order to occur. One can experience divine union while watching a sunset at the beach or from your terrace, taking a walk in the mountains or red wood forest. Divine union only requires the ability of the initiate to honor, themselves and whomever or whatever is around them. In a state of honor, magic is generated through the love of one's own I AM Presence, the Higher Self.

The experience of divine union is created when love from the Higher Self pours through one's body. As the love of 'All that Is' pours through one's energy field, this love blesses all who are present and offers others an opportunity to begin to wake up from the third dimensional mass conscious dream. As initiates transcend the Kumara of Fear, they begin to embody a state of divine union. Fear can be equated to the emotion that is experienced when one feels separated from God and the Higher Self. Once the experience of separation is transcended, the feeling of fear departs as one experiences divine union.

A state of divine union also requires that the masculine and feminine sides of an initiate come to a working balance within. It is the competition between the masculine and feminine or between the masculine and God, that is the root of the lack of balance required to sustain the state of divine union.

The Law of Drama

The law of Drama is closely linked to the law of Karma (the law of Cause and Effect) and the law of Dharma (Right Action) is the law of Drama.

The law of Drama expresses as the struggle that comes from the action right or wrong, on the way to the result. The law of Drama demonstrates that it is not the external result of an action which was of greatest significance but the inner character growth or decay that develops during the struggle.

The Law of Duality

Life in the physical body is preserved, physically and spiritually, under the impulse of the powerful will-to-be of the incarnated soul. This upon the magnetic power of the planetary life inherent in every atom of the form nature, by means of these atoms isolated and held by the law of Attraction in form. It is a projection of consciousness into an isolated form, created, occupied and in dwelt by a soul, by a living being. It is a peculiar aspect of isolation which conditions the physical body of the human or any living form, rendering it detached, coherent and temporarily living its own life in response to the imposition of the livingness of the incarnating Soul.

Two aspects of life and two forms of will or purpose are brought together. The higher type of energy is evolutionary the lower type of energy is involutionary in nature. This creates two aspects of livingness that of the Spirit of the Earth and that of the spiritual man. It is these conflicting forces which present the problem of dualism. The swing of the pairs of opposites is felt strongly when the soul is on the probationary path, joy and bliss then gloom and depression as the disciple swings back and forth between the dualities, astral in nature and sensuous in quality, not a quality of the soul. This causes separateness.

Duality is opposing forces of energy that play against one another through judgment and competition and so creating the ego as part of the personality. Looking at duality from occupying the middle golden line we can deal with the complexities. It is accepting and embracing duality in life that makes it possible for us to find this golden middle line in all our endeavors. As we live on this plane of duality we need to exercise the law of Balance to create a polarity of female/male, negative/positive energies to achieve harmony and integration. This is the first step towards enlightenment. The state of harmony, however, is not meant to be stagnant but is a constant slight motion in one way or the other though avoiding any extremes. See the law of Balance.

The Law of the Earth

No condition can be corrected or changed in the physical world without having the understanding, the use and the recognition of the love of the Ascended Hosts and Masters. The Great Seven Mighty Elohim. The more you remember to qualify your every thought, feeling and action with Love, the more love will teach you about itself and the more understanding you will have of the many powers of love. With the power of love present, in your electronic belt that surround you, of the Ascended Beings protecting you, you will not be at the mercy of the destructive forces. This is the law of the Earth. The Cosmic law does not allow the Ascended Beings to help you unless you recognize, accept and make conscious use of the power of their love, into all your affairs. This must be done of your own free will. As you keep charging the Hearts Flame of Love into the electronic circle around you, you increase the power into the reservoir by which you produce instant manifestation in your physical world. The more you do this the more the memory will come back to you of having had the use of this before.

The people of certain nations in the East have always been aware of and have accepted the Presence of the Ascended Beings, recognizing them to be the Elder Brothers of mankind constantly assisting life to be free. It is the confusion and the doubt and the incessant loud fast activities and demands in the western way of life that have created a veil making it difficult for most people to accept the existence of higher beings. The Ascended Masters are higher beings who have all gone through the incarnation process of life on this earth, who have evolved through the same experiences, trials and errors on the physical plane, to enlightenment and to existence on higher planes of being. Krishna, Moses, Jesus, Buddha are examples of the more widely known Masters or Avatars. There are many others less widely known.

The Law of Economy

This law of Economy causes matter always to follow the line of least resistance, and is the basis of the separate action of atomic matter. It governs matter, the opposite pole of spirit. Initiates must master this law before they can achieve liberation, or enlightenment.

The Law of Economy of Force

This is one of the three major Cosmic Laws. The law of Economy is the basic law of one pole, the negative aspect. This third cosmic law governs matter the opposite of spirit and causes matter to follow the line of least resistance. This law adjusts all that concerns the material and spiritual evolution of the cosmos with a rhythmic expenditure of force. This is done to the best possible advantage with the proper adjustment of equilibrium and with the necessary rate of rhythm. Unevenness of rhythm does not exist on the cosmic level. The person who aims at providing point of contact between conditions of chaos and those who work for constructive ends and order, should likewise use that most necessary factor of common sense in all activities.

For example, in a dual you do not just hit your opponent instead you use your opponent's force in order to strike back. Where this is done time is wisely distributed and energy is economized, something that one cannot do with zealousness. Zealousness does not rationalize nor does it know how to differentiate. This involves obedience to the law of Economy of Force, due to discrimination and a true sense of values. The Ascended Beings find a helper in an aspirant with such common sense, a dynamic way of thinking, seeing, relating and acting, with intuitive and rhythmic logic and inner knowing.

The law of Economy starts on the physical plane to the lower mental plane. On the higher spiritual planes it becomes the law of Love.

The Law of Education

We are all students and all teachers from the day we are born to the day we die. Knowledge is a divine aspect of the Creator and is gained through education. Life offers us limitless educational opportunities both academic and practical. All souls are in the process of education. This does not necessarily refer to the traditional book education only but more to the practical, emotional and spiritual education a soul goes through the school of life and experiences gained during each lifetime by its personal endeavors and relationships. This explains maturity found in younger children and immaturity in many adults as it is the soul position on the evolution ladder, that is meant here and which mostly reveals itself through the personality.

On the physical level, a fundamental change in the methods of teaching in the future is inevitable, where the emphasis will be laid upon the fact of soul existence on its own plane, its alignment with the lower self and for direct communication with the physical brain. The faculty of intuition will be developed and men and women will be taught to think, to control their mental body and to discover their full potential. Education will focus on the true science of linking up the integral parts of man and to link him in turn with his immediate environment and with the greater whole in which he has to play his part. One of the main immediate objectives must be the elimination of the competitive spirit and the substitution of the cooperative consciousness. The world itself is a great blending pot out of which the 'One Humanity' is emerging.

Through new methods of education, barriers will be removed. The fact that great art and literature have always belonged to the world is emphasized, confirming our similarities rather than differences, spiritual idealism and creative achievements. Two major ideas that should be taught are the value of the individual and the fact of the 'one humanity.' The effort of education to civilize the child will be to train and rightly direct its instincts, to develop and use its intellect correctly and elicit and develop the intuition. When these three faculties are developed and functioning correctly we will have a civilized, cultured and spiritually awakened human being. The adult will be instinctively correct, intellectually sound, and intuitively aware. The soul, the mind and the brain will function in the right relation to each other and as they should.

It is the responsibility of parents and educators to provide the child with an atmosphere of love and understanding, patience and courtesy plus to have regular ordered activities. This will encourage the child to grow without fear, shyness or timidity, accepting small duties and sharing of responsibility and likewise to be patient and courteous to all alike. An atmosphere of understanding is important so that the child is sure that the reasons and motives of his actions are recognized and the nature of his motivation is comprehended, even though parents or educators might not agree or approve of his actions. An educational system must be worked out that makes it possible for all barriers to be removed and prejudices of every kind eliminated, and a training given to the developing child to enable him or her to grow and live with harmony and goodwill.

The Law of Elevation

The law of Elevation is for individuals who have been elevated to be governed by soul laws who are welded together as a group by a united aspiration and objective. In the past successful groups were composed of kindred souls who are all thinking alike, none of whom think with intuition, who are governed by some school of thought, or because some central figure dominates all the rest, hypnotizing them into an instinctual static condition. This served the purpose perhaps for the teacher and the group but not that of the Divine.

The new groups consist of free souls, individual and developed souls, who recognize no authority but that of their own individual souls, and submerge their interests to the soul purpose of the group as a whole. Just as the achievement of an individual has, down the ages, served to raise the race of mankind, so a paralleling achievement in group formation will tend to raise humanity, still more rapidly. See also the law of Group Endeavor.

The Law of Energy

Because God is pure thought, energy is also pure thought. Spirit is energy in motion, and energy is the physical world manifests as e-motion, energy in motion. Energy > thought > action > manifestation. It is not, therefore, possible to dissipate energy. Energy does change forms, but is as spirit energy is eternal. Lack of energy does not exist. We have an inexhaustible reservoir of energy to draw upon something that we should always remember. Energy is neutral, The use of energy causes constructive or destructive movement.

The Law of Enthusiasm

An enthusiast is one who is possessed by God and celestial inspiration, full of rapturous intensity of feeling, in pursuit of a goal with passionate eagerness, proceeding from an intense conviction of the worthiness of an object. Enthusiasm is a soul quality.

This law of Enthusiasm indicates that which allows one to be filled with spirit which then, in turn may be used for purposes that can create greater expressions of spirit. Awareness indicates when one moves along in actions wherein new discoveries relating to self, new self-discoveries are made, one then purges oneself of the old and brings in the new energies of the discovery. Action increases enthusiasm. This awareness indicates that the word "enthusiasm" relates unto spirit within, and the spirit within is that which enhances the life-force factor. This awareness also indicates that those who use the law of Enthusiasm for destructive purposes are those who shall reap the whirlwind of devastation on many planes and many levels thereafter activating the law of Karma.

Awareness of this law indicates that essentially, when one begins to stagnate and move through life in a robot type of behavior pattern, one loses enthusiasm for life. Life then becomes mechanical in nature because even if one indulges in the thrills and desires nothing seems to change any more. One is bored. Nothing progresses. When one stagnates one loses more and more of the protective aura around the body and around the psyche. One loses vitality of the physical and spiritual body. When the vitality is depleted the aura tends to draw in the forces which result in illness or accident or further weakening of the bodies. This becomes likened unto an invitation to the higher forces, the so-called Lords of Karma, to take action to remove the entity from this plane.

This law makes it clear to us that it is desirable for us to strive always for higher achievements and to do that with great enthusiasm.

The Law of Essence

The law of Essence states that what is...IS, and what is, is not changed by any opinions or beliefs about it, but IS what it is, while it is.

This law states that actions and motives which are of the highest and the best quality, the most inclusive and encompassing, the most appropriate and essential, create those movements that lead to the Gate of Essence, behind which all things are exactly as they are, while they are. Essence is the ever-changing truth that was, is and forever shall be. The essence is the is-ness of what is happening at any moment regardless of the length of time included in that moment. This Awareness indicates that awareness of what "is" is total bliss and total union with the Godhead. The Sufis refer to the Essence in the human.

The Law of Essential Integrity

This law concerns the integrity and activity of the soul in form. This law has ten subsidiary laws with which the true healer must work. This law is important for healers as well as for those souls who are ill and might be seeking help from therapists and healers.

The healer must be trained to know the source of the problem of the one who seeks help, the innermost stage of thought and of desires, to know of the cause and the effect of the disease. The healer must achieve magnetic purity for the self through purity of life and must attain that dispelling radiance that shows itself when the centers in the head are linked. It is through this magnetic field when established that the radiation for healing goes forth. The healer must seek to link soul, heart, brain and hands and only then can the healer pour vital healing force upon the patient. This is known as magnetic work. It can cure the disease but it can also increase the evil state according to the knowledge and purity of the healer. When the healer has linked soul, brain, heart and auric emanation of the self, then the mere presence of the healer can feed the soul life of the patient. This is known as the work of radiation. For this the hands are not needed for the soul displays its power. The soul of patient responds likewise through the aura. The healer heals through love and not through the will. See also the law of Healing.

The Law of Evolution

An aspect of the law of Evolution is that achievement is ever followed by sacrifice and the giving of the greater for the lesser. This is the theme of the entire creative process and is the basic meaning of the phrase 'God is love,' for love signifies giving and sacrifice in this solar system. Therefore, forgiveness and sacrifice in order to save others is the keynote at this time. What is meant here is that the 'giving for' and 'sacrifice' involves right living upon the physical plane and not as often misinterpreted, the dying of the physical body as a sacrifice. It is the sacrifice day by day, in the process of daily living which can save the world. The sacrifice of selfish personal interests for the good of the whole and the giving up of one's practical life to the salvage of the world. It is living in order that others may live. When all this is understood correctly and practiced by humanity the new age will be realized and teachings of the true meanings of esoterism will be known.

In the total evolution of the spiritual man through physical incarnation during untold hundreds of lives, the entire process is simply one of expanding consciousness and of attaining sequentially and stage by stage an ever more inclusive awareness. The entire story of evolution is covered in a few words that Jesus Christ said: 'If any man shall do His will, he shall know.' In other words, doing precedes knowing because knowledge is gained through experiment and experience. We must keep in mind that space is an entity and the aphorism explains this 'In Him we live and move and have our being' and we must see ourselves in relation to this 'all-enveloping

Entity.' We are always moving in a world of energies that make an impact upon us from varying directions. Because completion is guaranteed so also is evolution. Evolution may be temporarily subverted but will always prevail. Evolution is a byproduct of knowledge which is itself a byproduct of Divine intelligence. Evolution is a constant rising towards the higher spheres, towards God, and when people are drab, hard and resistant it means that one is going in the opposite direction, regress rather than progress.

The Law of Example

The law of Example states that any person, concept or thing which is placed in a position of significance, may serve as an example for others to follow. Those who have served as examples of power, lust and greed, have helped to create the tragedies which they and their followers have spawned. Those who have served as examples of love, service and the sharing of their better parts, have helped to bring about freedom, beauty, joy and peace that has been allowed upon this plane. If we wish ourselves a better world and inner peace then all we need to do is to exemplify and portray the qualities of love, joy, peace and render service to others, particularly to the children who are searching for examples in their world.

The Law of Exclusion

This law of exclusion of contraction is the opposite of the law of Expansion. One becomes reductive in describing oneself as less than what all that is, one is either this or that, not this and not that, reducing oneself and one's world into oblivion. Reductiveness does not allow intrinsic aspects of our being to come forth and inhibits the material imagination that is a magical participation in life. This law denies the depth, the warmth, action, poetry, ambivalence, dreams of our secret being and longings. When this law of energies is activated all is denied, dreams, desires imagination and growth. See the law of Expansion.

The Law of Expansion

This law of a gradual evolutionary expansion of the consciousness in dwelling every form is the cause of the spheroidal form of every life in the entire solar system. This awareness indicates that the law of Expansion is that inclusion which results when the definition and description of a part or a situation is expanded to include something else. The law of Expansion is that which is never-ending as long as there is more which may be included by redescribing. Those who understand the law of Expansion will understand that they are more than a physical body, more than a name, more than a social being, more than a life of action, more than a center of a society, more than an observer and an observed, more than a symbol for humanity, more than the awareness of the earth and solar system, more than the confines of form: that they are all that is and all that can possibly be. Those who move from the law of Expansion into the law of Exclusion or Contraction would describe themselves as being something less than all that is. This being an exclusive law which describes them as being this, but not that; and this but not that until they are almost nothing at all in a universe of overwhelming forces. Beware of the law of Exclusion, lest you exclude yourself from all else into the oblivion of the bottomless pit. Any values must remain vulnerable and those that do not are dead. In other words this law demands that we are not singular about any of one thought. Imagination and dreaming are part of this law of expansion. The opposite of this law is when one becomes reductive and denies multiplicity of perspectives. See also the law of Exclusion which is the opposite of the law of Expansion.

The Law of Expectation

According to this law energy follows thought. We move toward but not beyond that what we can imagine. What we assume, expect or believe colors and creates our experiences and our world. By changing our thoughts and expectations, we can change without fail our experiences of every aspect of our lives. It is all in our mind. Our largeness and our smallness. The power of expectancy, while not a universal law, is a state of mind and of spirit that gives life to our creative powers. If you expect much, you will obtain much! If you expect little, you will get little! If you expect nothing, then you will receive nothing. Even if you are in a world of turmoil and confusion, practice abstract thought and activate your understanding of the laws to your own life so that your world can be one of peace, order and joy. Your world depends on how you choose to create it through your beliefs, your application of the universal laws and your expectancy.

The Law of Faith

The law of Faith is founded upon the recognition that we all know more than what we have read, heard or studied. We know more because WE are a part of the ALL.

We have a direct link to the universal wisdom, we just need to learn and to remember how to access this link. This we can do if we look within, listen, discern, and most of all, if we trust. We need to learn to develop more trust in our own deepest intuition and wisdom as the final arbiter and source of our decisions.

Faith being a vibration of the highest frequency will always prevail. Doubt never succeeds but Faith always does. Faith is the feeling of Light. It does not take faith it takes application. If you have faith, which is the feeling of light, it will act more rapidly but if you make your application, the law is compelled to act for you. Faith is the presentiment of knowledge. Like a motive force, faith intensifies the energy. Despair is the death of faith. When faith is knowledge then despair is the death of knowledge.

The Law of Fixation

This is one of the seven laws of the Solar System. By means of The law of Fixation the mind controls and stabilizes. This is the governing law on the mental plane. 'As a man thinks so is he.' According to his thoughts are his desires and acts and so results his future. He fixes for himself the resultant karma. This law governs the crystallization of all forms prior to their shattering in the process of evolution. The word fixation implies the capacity of the thinker to shape his own destiny. His desires and acts are in accordance with his thoughts and so is his future. He fixes for himself the resultant karma. He fixes his future through his thoughts. It is the concentration and the focus on the goal. Wherever we have our focus and whatever we concentrate on we energize and bring into form. This law also governs the time of rebirth.

The Law of Flexibility

This law involves a pragmatic acceptance of the present moment. It demands that we accept ourselves, others and current circumstances. That we do not exercise a rigid resistance of what is occurring at the moment. It requires an alert and expansive state of awareness and embracing and making constructive use of the moment. Stumbling blocks become stepping stones and problems become opportunities. Everything serves our highest good if we can learn to make good use of it. The serenity prayer used by Alcoholics Anonymous and other twelve step programs reflect this law. 'God grant me the serenity to accept the things I cannot change, the courage to change the things I can, and the wisdom to know the difference.' This prayer is drawn from Buddha's writings.

The Law of Forgiveness

This law works with the energy of openness, and the ability to see all as love, so one may dispense with the unnatural feeling of getting even or revenge. The old energy of an eye for an eye keeps the vibrations of a person very low. To forgive, to release old stored anger allows the law of grace to intercede and dispense with amounts of karma an individual has stored on the astral level. Non-violence is the natural outgrowth of the law of forgiveness and love. All good comes from forgiveness. It is a truth that the continuation of the human species is due to man's being forgiving. Forgiveness is holiness. By forgiveness the universe is held together. Forgiveness is the might of the mighty. Forgiveness gives peace of mind. Forgiveness and gentleness are the soul qualities of the self-possessed and represent eternal virtue. One is only forgiven when one forgives. Failure to forgive one's self or others is a violation of this law.

Forgiveness is healing and fills one with light and perfection. When forgiveness is sincere, the individual will find his world reordered and filled with all good things as if by magic. But it must be remembered that unless a discord is forgotten it is not forgiven because you cannot release yourself from it until it is out of your consciousness. As long as you remember an injustice and harbor an inner disturbed feeling you have not really forgiven either the person or the condition. When forgiveness is complete, the emotional body experiences peace, freedom, health and vitality.

Forgiving someone does not necessarily mean that you have to like the person or have to be friendly with him or her, but it does mean that you have to wish them well and let them go on their way with no anger or resentments.

The Law of Freedom

The law of Freedom allows that movement which gives all living beings the space to expand and grow in their ability to function in a manner that will allow others their freedom and space to grow, in order to free still others. Freedom is not a final state of being. It is an ever-expanding action of giving each other the space to create spaces for others, to create more spaces for still others yet to come. Freedom may be helped or hindered by laws, definitions, principles, descriptions, disciplines and boundaries. Universal Laws free each and every one. Any law that fails to do that, is subject to the rule of a still greater law. No one is free until each is free and all are freeing each other.

The Violet Consuming Flame is the law of Freedom to the Earth and is the law and the authority that governs the action of mankind in the centuries yet to come. It is said that the Violet Consuming Flame must be intensified upon this planet for the next ten thousand years in order to keep mankind purified long enough to let the Divine Plan manifest its reality and blessings for the future. One can purify oneself with the Violet Flame through one's own mind, thoughts and imagination. One imagines oneself standing and being completely enveloped, surrounded and purified by the Violet Flame, cleansing negative emotions such as fear, anger, greed, selfishness or any other vice that one might have. Do this for a few minutes as often as you can remember. Know that as soon as you consciously make your decree it manifests on the psychic level. The fact that it is invisible does not make it less effective. When you have faith and you repeatedly make your decrees you will experience definite positive changes in your life on the physical plane.

The Law of Free Will

We are a privileged species to have been given intelligence and the free will for freedom of choice. We are free to choose our direction. Predestination determines what our destiny in life would be, if we choose to fulfill that destiny. This law works the same for every one of us regardless who we are and no one has the right to infringe on this freedom of will. Anyone who robs any individual the freedom of choice is violating this universal law.

The law of Free Will states that divine will grants each individual the right to direct and pursue his or her life and the quality of that life, so long as he or she does not violate this same right of others. A right that excludes the rights of others is other than divine. Although through God's grace we have been given free will the only purpose of free will is to surrender it back to the Creator. Free will is a learning tool of the lower mind, the ego. We are absolutely free to choose opposition to God during the process of spiritual growth, however, opposition to God is a violation of the universal law of One. Free will when properly exercised simply allows each soul to grow at its own pace and in its own way, choosing its own path, reflecting the basic personality of the soul as assigned by God. This is also a good reason why no one has the right to exercise any force on another individual in spiritual development or change in their belief system. Everything must be achieved through the individual free will. See also the law of Choice.

The Law of Friction

This law governs the heat aspect of any atom, the radiation of an atom, and the effect of that radiation on any other atom.

The Law of Fulfillment

This law has to do more with the work of the Ashrams rather than with us. Part of the service rendered by members of an Ashram is to make way for new aspirants. They do this by hastening their own progress and moving forward so that they are admitted to a higher Ashram leaving a vacancy for new disciples which are promptly filled. By fulfillment is meant the full compliance of a disciple with the service demands upon the outer plane. When these demands are met and the service is effective then the outer effectiveness produces inner effectiveness.

The Law of Garment of Light

Youth is a garment of light. Light is a garment of knowledge. Water is a garment of health. Life without virtues is like a garden without flowers or trees without fruit. The beginning of all things is spirit. The beginning of spirit is love. The zenith of the spirit is wisdom. The end of all things is truth that brings freedom. There is only an end where all contradictions cease. There is only a beginning where all is in accord. If the heart does not feel, the beautiful cannot come. If the mind does not think, the great will remain unknown.

One can through regular meditation, concentration and decree establish a garment of light in one's aura as a protective device against all negative and adversary vibrations. See also the law of Freedom.

The Law of Gender

This law embodies the truth that gender is manifested in everything. The masculine and the feminine is ever at work on all planes of causation. Gender manifests on all three planes of causation the physical plane, the mental plane and the spiritual plane. The law is the same on all planes but on the higher planes, it takes higher forms of manifestation. This law works in the direction of generation, regeneration, and creation. All life forms contain within them the two elements of gender the masculine and the feminine. On the great physical plane, the sexes of all species are manifested as male and female and the role they play in sexual reproduction. On the great mental plane, gender manifests as masculine and feminine energies that exist within each and every person. Every male has its female element, and every female has its male element within. On the great spiritual plane gender manifests as the Father Mother principle of the Infinite Omnipresent God in whose mind the universe is conceived and firmly held. It is written 'In Him we live, move and have our being.' When balance and learning reach a critical mass, the personality achieves the merger of God, and will see self as neither male nor female but as the one blended Self.

The Law of Giving

Giving and receiving are part of the exchange that perpetuates the energy flow of the universe. As we are receptive to the premise of giving that which we desire to receive, the abundance of the universe is perpetuated in our lives. We must give in order to receive, and we must receive in order to give. The energy of each is equal, and the universe will respond to either with a pull of the energy of the other.

Some people say, 'Well I do give but I seldom see any sign of return.' There is a right way and a wrong way to give. There is careless impulsive giving, and there is careful, scientific giving. When we give impulsively we are retarding progress, we are wasting our substance. Where we give to one who doesn't put forth the effort to help himself, we need not expect a good return. Nature does not support a parasite or a loafer, but she gives her energy to the ones who are struggling forward. She lets the parasite and the loafer see that she will help if they put forth the effort to help themselves. But with us, if we support a loafer in what he is in, how can we expect any good returns? Rather the loafer becomes arrogant and demanding for more and more relief, until we wonder where and when it will end.

After giving, our next step is to prepare to receive the response or results of our giving and to receive, as the law states, 'good measure, pressed down, shaken together, and running over.' This is the exciting part, because our preparation shows our active faith. Instead of rocking and waiting, we are prepared and working. This in turn enlarges our view. It stimulates our interest, it disperses our doubt and fear, and energizes our power of reception. The key to this law is that we are continually drawing into our life what we give and expect. Therefore what we receive will be in accordance with our actions and intentions. If you want smiles and kindness from others then give smiles and kindness to others. If you want help from angels then find someone who is less privileged than you are and share your light with this person, your actions will be reflected in the invisible world and it will be a call for entities to come and do likewise for you.

The Law of Goodness

Although the universal law of Balance applies in true reality, there is nothing outside of goodness or of Godliness. Therefore all there is, is good all there is, is God.

The Law of Goodwill

Knowledge of this law will help those who have feelings of hopelessness when thinking about the course of world events. By viewing life in terms of energy, we understand that our higher self coupled with our thought-mind creates energy and action-energy solidifies this thought into matter or results. In an energy relationship there is always a positive, creating side and a negative receiving side of that creative relation. This is simply how the world works. The will-to-good is the positive, creative impetus, which when received, makes the manifestation of goodwill possible. We are either mentally polarized or emotionally polarized and only those who are mentally polarized can begin to appropriate this energy through will on the mental plane. When this is fully comprehended, we begin to realize why the manifestation of goodwill is not more widespread.

An initiate states that it is absolutely essential that the will-to-good be unfolded by the disciples of the world, so that goodwill can be expressed by the 'rank and the file' of mankind. The will-to-good of the world 'knowers' is the magnetic seed of the future.' Our mental capacity today readily contacts those ideas that constitute the purpose behind the form. We have the ability to mentally construct a happening, and see it through to completion. This is will-to-good. The desire of one to create a loving scenario of 'goodwill' is another but related action. The will-to-good is always an education process where the recipients are left with the freedom of choice to receive the idea or not. The responsibility for expanding the amount of goodwill in the world lies directly on the shoulders of the intelligentsia of the world.

In the goodwill process it is the creative, idea or problem solving individuals who are directly responsible for creating goodwill. The 'rank and file' of humanity simply does not yet possess the mental capacity to evoke the process, even though many are able to participate in the process. This knowledge should fill the responsible group with a greater amount of hope and assurance, because they have the power to generate goodwill in their every day routine solving of problems. An initiate says: 'When the majority of the inhabitants of the earth are being rapidly oriented towards good, towards righteousness, as the Bible expresses it, and the bulk of human beings are inclined towards goodwill then ill health will persistently, even if only gradually, disappear and die out and finally become non-existent. Slowly, very slowly this is already happening.'

The Law of Grace

Karma when properly discharged leads to a total release of obligation. This law can waive the law of Karma. When applied, this law allows a person to receive more than one deserves or works for provided it is in the highest good for all. When called upon, this law allows the person to send another a healing, to do soul talk or to use divine decree, and not suffer the consequences of karma interference with the receiver's soul plan. The wording to insert in the request is 'Under the law of Grace.' Another aspect of this law is to be of higher vibration to consistently live in grace. i.e. A loving person who works diligently sending world healing to Mother Earth and all life on her body, and focusing so much on this activity, will find that life will run more smoothly than otherwise due to the law of Grace. This condition, however, cannot be taken for granted nor abused or it will leave one.

The law of Grace states that any Divine Being can apply the law of Mercy to grant a pardon to one who has made a mistake, so that the Karma may be set aside. But such an act of pardon is entirely at the discretion of the Divine Being, and though individuals may request and seek, or beg, they have no right to demand grace, mercy or forgiveness, when other karmic justice is their due.

The Grace of God does not descend upon us i.e. it does not come to us for no reason. We first have to earn it. We have to lift ourselves up to God and then the Grace of God will meet us and lift us up.

The Law of Gratitude

Although the creator allows us to create through absolute principle of Grace, gratitude is a function of free will. Compliance with this law does increase our heart's desire and heals old patterns. Refer also the universal law of Increase. The law of Gratitude is that sense of satisfaction in knowing that energy, which has been given, receives its certain reward according to its nature. Energy that is given moves out on that curved and unequal line and when extended far enough, can only return to its source bearing its appropriate gifts. It governs the process of petal unfoldment and so it demonstrates a triple law. The law of Solar Heat, the law of Solar Light and the law of Solar Fire.

The Law of Gravitation

The law of Gravitation shows itself in one aspect as the power, and the stronger urge that a more vital life may have upon the lesser, such as the power of the spirit of the earth, the planetary entity, to hold all physical forms to itself and prevent their scattering. This is due to the heavier vibration, the greater accumulative force, and the aggregated tamasic lives of the body of the planetary entity. This force works upon the negative or the lowest aspect of all physical forms.

The law of Gravity shows itself also in the response of the soul of all things to the greater Soul in which the lesser finds itself. This law affects the two lowest forms of divine life but not the highest. It emanates in the first instance from the physical sun and the heart of the sun. This force works upon the negative or lowest aspect of all physical forms. The law shows itself in the response of the Soul of all things to the greater Soul in which the lesser finds itself.

The Law of Group Endeavor

This law defines the multiplying of energy one creates when acting with like minded individuals to form a group effort to pray, to manifest, to do light work, for the good of all concerned, or even to create degrees of control which we define as evil or black magic. Where the efforts of an individual may equal one unit, the efforts of two praying or healing for a common goal with equal energy will effect the energy of twenty units instead of the sum total of two. With three, the resultant energy explodes further. The longer pure thought (the exclusion of any other thought) of one's desired goal is held in the mind, the more powerful the result. Holding a pure thought for an increment of time is the beginning lesson of manifestation.

The Law of Group Life

The law of Group Life comes into expression when one fulfills with love family, social, national and global obligations, when one thinks of the wider terms of humanity itself. This is also known as the law of Brotherhood. Brotherhood is a group quality. Questions of self such as 'Will my action tend to the group good?' Will the group suffer or hurt if I do this or that?' should be always foremost in our minds. Abiding by these actions will gradually become part of our human consciousness and our civilization will adjust itself to these new conditions. All aspects of life are interdependent and when one proceeds to full expression then all members of the group benefit.

Margo Kirtikar Ph.D.

The Law of Group Progress

This law is also known as the law of Elevation. The symbol is the mountain and the goat standing at the summit with the astrological sign of Capricorn. All hard places can be surmounted and the summit reached by the Divine Goat—a symbol meaning Group Effort. The ray energy is progressive energy of the seventh ray, the evolving factor.

The Law of Growth

Spiritual growth is mandatory and infinite. What attention is placed on a specific thought-course of action-causes it to grow, to increase. Lack of attention on a specific thought whether positive or negative, causes it to decrease which, however, is also to be interpreted as growth. Refer here also to the law of Paradox.

The Law of Happiness

The law of Happiness states that it is not what you are, what you do, or what you have that determines happiness, but how you feel about who you are, what you do, what you have and more important, what you do with what you have. Many people spend their entire life chasing after happiness and never find it. Many seek their happiness through other persons or objects in their life, unaware that true happiness comes from within and has much more to do with the attitude you have about yourself, life, your role in life and relationship with life and your fellow humans. When you have arrived to this awareness then you will not need to look for happiness because joy and happiness become a part of you.

The secret of all success and happiness is to manifest in your own behavior whatever you would like to receive from others.

The Law of Harmony

The law of Harmony and Agreement states that efforts to manipulate, trick or force another to behave in harmony and agreement will only disrupt previously established areas of harmony and agreement. Yet, even between the most hostile enemies, some area of harmony and agreement can be discovered when there is an agreement to discover these areas. Ever increasing harmony and agreement grows from the mutual agreement to discover more areas of agreement. This law is based on discovering rather than on the enforcement of harmony and agreement.

The Law of Healing

The law of Healing concerns the ability of one to channel energy also referred to as Holy Spirit, Prana and Chi, which radiates from the Source, the Higher Power or from whom we call God. The purpose of this channeled energy is to either improve self or another by removing blockages or instilling the sacred energy that pulsates from the Source. With intent or technique we may send this energy to the past, present or future. Hands on healers who are effective in healing have brain waves at 7.8 Hz—the same as the earth's pulse beat. Their brain waves are in sync with the earth's beat, at the time the healing is performed. Another aspect of this law is the ability of one in the third dimension to heal self by that which triggers a leap in faith.

All initiates of the Ageless Wisdom are basically healers, though all may not heal the physical body. The reason for this is that all souls that have achieved any measure of true liberation are transmitters of healing energy. Since all disease is the result of inhibited soul life, the art of the healer consists in releasing the soul so that its life can flow freely through the form. There are three ways in which healing can be brought about, and all three have their value, depending upon the point of evolution of the subject being healed. The first is where the patient is passive and methods are used which gradually cure disease, help to eliminate undesirable conditions and restore vitality. All homeopathic schools of healing are included in this method. The second way is that of the modern psychologist who seeks to correct the attitude of mind, inhibitions and

Flowing with Universal Laws

neurotic complexes that bring about the disease. This is a positive and active method and it is a step in the right direction. The combination of the psychology with the outer physical treatment is sound and right. The third and newest method, however, is that of calling positive activity in the subject's own soul. This is where the true healing is brought about when the life of the soul can flow without any hindrance or obstacles that block it. In this case the soul can vitalize the form with its own power and so eliminate all congestion that causes the disease.

Disease differs in humanity depending on the point of evolution of the individual. The healer must be able to make a distinction and to gauge the point of evolution that has been reached by the patient. Some diseases the healer must deal with through the mind plane, others require a concentration of the emotional energy and in other cases the healer need only to be the transmitter of pranic energy to the etheric body of the patient via the healer's etheric body. Any man or woman prompted by the incentive to serve, who thinks and loves can be a healer. Every initiate is a healer and the more advanced initiates automatically heal whom ever is within their aura. See also the law of Essential Integrity and the law of Thought.

The Law of Higher Will

From the perspective of our separate self and smaller will, it is normal for us to act on the basis of our own desires and preferences. When we can, however, surrender our lower self and will, to the guidance of a higher will and dedicate our actions for the highest good of ALL concerned, we feel an inspired glow at the center of our life. The higher will is from the Divine, the lower will is the personality will.

The Law of Honesty

The law of Honesty requires that we see things as they are, without an attempt to alter that which is seen, either for purposes of advantage or out of fear. To recognize, to accept and to express our authentic interior reality lies at the heart of honesty. Only when we are honest with ourselves can we speak or act honestly with anyone else. In the sense of integrity, honesty entails acting in line with higher laws despite negative impulses to the contrary.

We don't need to be punished for breaking spiritual law or higher laws. The act itself is the punishment and sets into motion subtle forces whose natural consequences we cannot escape any more than we can escape the force of gravity. When we allow our fear to stop us from expressing our true feelings and needs, we are being dishonest with ourselves and this drains us from our energy and spirit. The law of Hierarchy is that by which the entire life is founded, that by which the world progresses and that upon which evolution is built. Hierarchy and Leadership are affirmed upon the Cosmic Law.

The Law of Honor

This law requires one to honor oneself along with all other life forms. In embracing the law of Honor, one embodies 'real love' and releases any remaining codependent patterns with others based on illusionary love, glitter or glamour. In embracing a state of honor, one chooses not to harm another either consciously or unconsciously or any plane of reality. In a state of honor, the vibration of harmlessness is maintained within an initiate's field. A state of honor recognizes that all aspects of Godliness are equal and that even the unconscious anti Christ souls are a part of the Creator and honors them as such. It is from the act of self honor that one does not allow another to harm the self. Through self honor, one does whatever it takes to cause others to understand that abusive and violent patterns of behavior be they physical, emotional or mental are not acceptable in their presence.

The Law of Humility

The opposite of humility is selfish pride. The central feature of pride is enmity. Enmity, or animosity, may be pitted against persons or Groups in society. Pride leads to contentions and strife, causes divisions and destroys unity through selfishness, greed and envy. Humility, gratitude and camaraderie serve as primary antidotes to dispel pride. As difficult and as fraught with danger as it is, the spiritual challenge is for man to let go all that he thinks he knows, so that a much deeper wisdom might emerge. This wisdom is one that is born not of having definite answers, but rather being willing to live with questions that cannot be answered. Out of this shift of perspective, can come a powerful humility and a profound sense of compassion for the struggle of others to find their own answers, an openness to truth in whatever form it happens to come and access to the very core of Life's deepest mysteries.

Sometimes humility is confused with lack of self esteem. Humility does not mean the absence of self confidence or the absence of knowledge that each of us has great worth. Humility can be manifested in a meek giant. The very best example of humility is when a powerful King takes on the role of a servant. The attitude of self-discipline, strength in meekness, and the heart to serve, will make children strong, confident and capable as they meet a hostile world.

The Law of Identity

This law pertains to the individual right of all to create one's own beingness. It applies to the time spent between incarnations as well as third dimension, our dimension, incarnational experiences. When one merges with the Great Central Sun-God, one still may separate to accomplish something and will possess an individual identity.

The Law of Impartiality

Spirit is divinely unaware of intrinsic difference between each of its thoughts, that which we perceive. Properties of the spirit are equally accessible to all. Each thought is inherently equal and of like value.

The Law of Increase

This law enables you to be lifted up and unconsciously touch the law of Increase and gain from its blessings. What you have created unconsciously or accidentally can be stimulated to increase. Increase can be obtained through praise. The act of praise alone can move mountains. This law is connected to the law of Praise. Praise is complementary to faith. Whereas faith is wisdom and understanding, praise is the application of that understanding. Faith is the boiler that holds a substance of power, whereas praise is the fuel that generates that power into an active force. Faith without praise is like a cold boiler, an innert mass of machinery. It may be nice to look at or talk about but it has no more value than a conversation piece. Praise is a stimulant of the mind. It magnetizes all the good around you. It transforms that good into usable, visible substances.

A prime biblical example of this, is the story of Jesus when he had some five thousand hungry souls to feed. He had five loaves of bread and a few fishes, yet he started action by praising the little at hand. You know the story. Jesus said that what he did we could do also. How can it be done? When you learn to take what you have and build on it, not in scorn and condemnation, but with praise and gratitude, you are working the law and the universe will give increasing abundance. Work with praise and faith and you will benefit from the law of Increase.

The spirit in which you act, for self or for others, is the key to this law. The seed-the spirit-in which you think, speak or act is sown in your inner self and there it grows. Every negative

Flowing with Universal Laws

word or thought, such as criticism or doubt, is a weed seed. In some way it is based on fear, distrust or other destructive attitude. Pull those weeds and throw them out! Better still, do not plant them at all in the first place! Your purpose, sincerity and willingness are the three areas to concentrate on to activate the law of Increase. The key to getting in the flow of a Universal Law is to apply the law. Whatever you want in life, apply that in your thoughts, words and acts toward yourself and others. It will grow and return to you as the "fruits" of your efforts.

The Law of Inertia

This law represents one of the qualities of nature, of 'prana' or of vital etheric energy. The three qualities are inertia, activity and rhythm. In Sanskrit known as Tamas, Raja and Sattva. Inertia is not only psychological in nature. The qualities of matter or substance are involved. Inertia is the slowest and lowest aspect of material substance and is called in the eastern philosophy, the quality of tamas. Inertia has to be transmuted into a higher quality, the activity of the rajastic quality that leads later on to the highest quality of rhythm or sattva. Sattva is the rhythm of life under which the Hierarchy operate and which vibrate in harmony with human need and hierarchical response. Inertia is not a desirable state to be in because it is not in harmony with life. Other words for inertia are sluggishness, idleness, passiveness, inactivity and listlessness, all of which are of the lowest vibration level and are undesirable because they hinder growth and consciousness unfoldment.

The Law of Infinite Energy

Energy has an ultimate Source. There is an Ultimate Intelligence, Infinite Consciousness, Universal Energy, the "All There Is," —God— which is totally infused with, and whose Purpose is the exercise of Love, Wisdom and Power. We call this "Universal Quint Essence." We are also each conduits of that Source. The degree to which you are aligned with Universal Quint Essence," the higher the quality of your life.

Modern exoteric science has proved that there is nothing in the whole of the manifested universe but energies, in some relationship, each vibrating at a particular frequency. The esoteric science acknowledges seven streams of energy, whose interaction, at every conceivable frequency, creates the solar systems, galaxies and universes. The movement of these seven rays of energy, in spiraling cycles, draws all being into and out of manifestation and colors and immerses it with their own individual qualities and character. This is the case be it a grain of sand, human being or solar system. The rays are of particular types of energy, the emphasis being on the quality which that energy demonstrates. There are, therefore, seven ray types of people. The three primary rays of aspect are: 1st ray of Power, Will or Purpose, 2nd ray of Love-Wisdom and 3rd ray of Active Creative Intelligence. The secondary rays of attribute are the 4th ray of Harmony through Conflict or Beauty or Art, the 5th ray of Scientific Knowledge, the 6th ray of Idealism or Devotion, and the 7th ray of Ceremonial Order or Magic Ritual or Organization. All of us are basically governed by five ray forces. The ray of the soul, which remains the same for countless incarnations, the personality ray which varies from life to life until all the qualities are developed, the ray governing the astral-emotional body, the ray of the physical body including the brain, and the ray of the mind. These vary cyclically. Each ray works through one chakra and together they determine the physical structure and appearance, the emotional nature and the quality of the mental body. Our attitudes of mind, our strengths and weaknesses are in accordance with our ray types. For the greater part of our evolutionary experience on this earth the rays of the personality control our life, but when we are two thirds of the way along the path, the soul ray begins to dominate and express itself through the being. Knowledge of one's rays provides insight to one's weaknesses and strengths, bridges and barriers between oneself and others. Those on similar rays have the same outlook and approach to life while those on different rays find it difficult to understand one another. The more one acquires the positive attributes of all rays the easier one can communicate with others regardless of the differences in ray energies.

The Law of Infinity

The Creator is limitless, therefore, so are we. The abilities of the Creator are limitless, and therefore our abilities are limitless too. As there exists a spark of the Creator in each of us, the Creator manifests on the physical level through each one of us.

The Law of Initiation

The law of Initiation is an expansion of consciousness that leads to a growing recognition of the inner realities. It is equally the recognition of a renewed sense of the need for change and the wise engineering of these needed changes so that real progress can be made. The consciousness is expanded and becomes more generously and divinely inclusive and there is a fresh and more potent control by the soul as it increasingly assumes the direction of the life of the individual, of a nation and of the world.

Initiation is when a man has passed out of the human kingdom into the spiritual kingdom and has entered upon the life of the spirit. Each initiation marks the passing of a pupil in the Hall of Wisdom into a higher class, the shining through of the inner fire, and the realization of the increasing unity with all that lives. It is a growing capacity to see and to hear on all planes. Initiation is where vision is possible of the eternal now, where past, present and future exist as one. Initiation gives a man the key to all information in graduated sequence and it leads from one state of consciousness into another until expansion reaches a point where the self embraces all selves. The initiate will know when the event occurs and needs no one to tell him or her of it. It is quite possible for one to be functioning on the physical plane actively with world service with no recollection of having gone through an initiation process in a previous life. The mark of an initiate is his lack of interest in himself and his personal fate.

Since the fact of initiation has been grasped by many, it has been possible today to reveal that initiation is a group event as it is the nature of the soul to be group conscious, with no individual ambitions or interests. Every step upon the path of initiation increases group recognition. As the initiate proceeds from one initiation to another and penetrates deeper into the heart of the Mysteries, in company with those who are working with him towards the same point of evolution and goal, the more he or she is aware that he or she is not alone and that it is a joint effort that is being made. No one is admitted into an Ashram of Christ or the Hierarchy until such times that one thinks and lives in terms of group relationships and activities. This should not be misunderstood to mean that one should form little groups, as was the case in the Piscean age. Ashrams exist with disciples an initiates at all points of evolutionary development and degrees, and all work together in unison within their differentiated ranks, for each degree stands alone and yet united with all the others.

The initiatory process is the result of the activity of three energies. The energy that is generated by the disciple as he or she seeks to serve humanity. The energy made available to the disciple as he or she succeeds in building the bridge of light, the antahkarana, and the energy of the hierarchical Ashram into which he or she is being integrated. The Path of Initiation includes long periods of search, detachment, pain and of revelations producing tension, fusion and energy projection. Initiation is not given to anyone, it is the recognition of the Lighted Way that indicates readiness for initiation. The initiate enters into the light, which penetrates his nature according to his or her development at any one point of time or space and enables him or her to see the unseen on the basis of the newly acquired knowledge. Each initiation dims the light already acquired and immerses the initiate in a higher light. Each initiation enables one to perceive an area of divine consciousness so far unknown. Initiation is a process of excessive hard work, a graded series of liberation allowing the initiate greater freedom to proceed further on the Way, learning to work behind the scenes, unrecognized, unknown, unacclaimed and receiving no rewards and sacrificing the individual identity in the identity of the Ashram.

The Law of Initiative

All action occurs as a direct result and in direct proportion to the initiative of each Soul. The energy initiative brings about evolution. See the law of Initiation.

The Law of Integration

This law represents the integration of the Soul and personality in the human. Through the use of the mind the personality makes contact with the Soul and so become integrated in the three worlds. The personality is the integration of the physical, the emotional and the mental worlds in one. Integration with the Soul with the personality is achieved through the building of what is known in Sanskrit as the Antakharana Bridge or the Rainbow Bridge, to connect with the Soul, the plane of intuition and the spiritual world. The goal of all development is integration—integration as a personality, integration with the Soul, integration with the Hierarchy, integration with the Whole, until complete unity and identification has been achieved.

The Law of Intelligence

All intelligence is divine. To increase our intelligence level depends solely on our connection with the Creator. The nearer we are to the higher realms of Spirit the higher the level of our intelligence as we connect with the divine intelligence of the Cosmos that has all knowledge.

The Law of Intention

When one's intention is held in the mind and action of the physical effort does not follow, people create false impressions of self. One thinks self is good or better than actions prove. Energy must follow intention for that which is perceived as good to happen. When an act of kindness is performed and intention is such that one wishes to be recognized for goodness, or has underlying motivation which is not of the higher order, higher rewards will not be forthcoming. Intention and effort must be of the higher vibration to gain or create spiritual accomplishment and reward. If a person gives a promise to another to do something and has an intention to do so, but does not follow through with action, this becomes a lie, a breaking of one's word violates the law and creates karma. In other words it is not enough to think of doing good and to leave it at that. Action must follow the thought for it to hold good.

The Law of Interdependence

Inter-dependence is a basic law of our Cosmos. Nothing exists independent of anything or anyone else. When we enter into a consciousness of interdependence, a consciousness of equality of being we are in harmony with this law. Meister Eckhart says: "One creature sustains another and enriches the other and that is why all creatures are interdependent." Physicists like Fritjof Capra, biologists like Lewis Thomas and ecologists like Jacques Cousteau all recognize inter-dependence as a basic law of our Cosmos. "Two persons who sit together in the same room are exchanging water and vapor within thirty minutes. This is interdependence." To take a deep breath is to breathe in some of the breath that our ancestors breathed be it, Jesus, Leonardo da Vinci or Mozart. Scientist Brian Swimme confirms this. "This is interdependence. Every square mile of soil on our earth contains particles from every other square mile of soil on our earth." says biologist John Storer. "This is interdependence. Compassion and interdependence is already in the universe, we do not have to invent it new."

One needs to learn to be independent in order to be able to be interdependent and not live one's life dependent on others or on circumstances.

The Law of Intuition

The intuition is on the fourth dimension, the Soul plane. The more one integrates the soul in one's life and activities the more constant and active is the intuition. We can only get in touch with our own source of intuition and wisdom when we no longer depend upon the opinion of others for our sense of identity or worth. Do we value and trust our own intuition, or do we value and transfer authority to the opinions of others over our own inner feelings? Our intuition becomes more profound when we claim our own sacred identity.

Sometimes instinct or inner voices originating from the lower astral level are mistaken for intuition and caution is advisable here. Many of us have experienced contact with our intuition sporadically or accidentally but we can, through the practice of regular meditation, solitude and silence, establish a permanent contact so that we are constantly guided by our intuition which has universal knowledge and can never be wrong. Once we have consciously made contact with our intuition through soul culture, we will be able to better differentiate between instinct and other inner voices and the intuition.

The Law of Isolation/Limitation

In this law we are given the clue to that which will ultimately sweep disease from the earth. When one is sick it is important to remember that one is not enduring alone and in isolation but that one is sharing the fate of the majority of humans. A right handling of ill health is a major factor in breaking down separateness and a sense of aloneness and isolation. That is why the effects of bad health, when rightly handled, lead to a sweetening of the disposition and a broadening of the sympathies. Sharing and a sense of general participation has usually to be learnt the hard way—such is the law. When the majority of the inhabitants of the earth are being rapidly oriented towards good, towards righteousness and all are inclined toward goodwill, then ill health will persistently even if only gradually disappear and finally become non existent.

The Law of Inverse Proportions

Also known as the law of Longevity. One need not die if the pranic life force is not lost but increased and drawn from the Cosmic source, conquering death and fate. The span of life is related to the rate of breathing. If the span of life is 120 years and the normal person breathed 21,600 times per day, that is 15 respirations per minute. If the rate of breathing is 18 per minute, however, the span of life will be about 96 years. If because of poor living habits and needless expenditure of energy the average rate of breathing is 30 per minute, the life span will be only 60 years. If the rate is slowed through yogi practices and self control to an average of only 5 respirations per minute the life span will be 360 years. If it is one per minute, the life span will increase to 1800 years. If the rate of breathing is reduced to zero, the life span becomes infinity. The secret of longevity lies in the technique of diverting the breathing to the subtle channels and centers. See also the law of Respiration.

The Law of Justice

Also known as the law of Exchange. The Law of Justice is likened unto scales in balance in which that which is heavy on one side must be balanced by that which is equally heavy on the other side. Thus, when one human violates another, the heavier the violation is, the heavier must be the balancing weight. This is related unto the law of Karma.

All things in time come into balance. When one puts on a heavy karma, one may help remove that karma by lightening the load of another who has been violated by that karma, if possible, or by lightening the load of someone who has an equally heavy load. It is simply a matter of weights and measures and this is the Cosmic law of Balance, Justice and Karmic Accounts. This law also gives us the sense for the existence of fairness in the world. No deed goes unnoticed, whether good or bad. Everything comes to a balance in one way or another in spite of the fact that this might not be visible to us or apparent at any one time. Refer also to the law of Karma.

On the spiritual level justice consists in taking one thing and giving something of equal value in exchange. The most valuable thing that we have to give is our life. If we give our life, our love and our attention, we can get anything we want from the cosmos. We work on the physical level and get money as compensation. The same is true on the spiritual level. As an example let's say I want to help someone but it turns out wrong and I hurt this person instead of helping. I would be punished on the physical level for that according to human laws, the higher powers cannot interfere on the physical level, but on a spiritual level I would be rewarded generously because of my good intentions and effort. Actions and motivations of the soul are under two different jurisdictions. If my intentions are evil in character and my actions on the physical level give the impression of being good, I might be rewarded by human laws on the physical level. However, on a higher spiritual level I will be called to justice and I will have to make good in one way or another for the imbalance that I caused.

The Sirian Law of Karma

This law is the synthesis of the system of Sirius and predicates the effect the Sirian system has on our solar system. Each of the two systems is independent in time and space and manifestation. We have no effect on our parent system but very definite effects are felt in our system through causes arising in Sirius. These causes when experienced as effects are called by us the law of Karma, which law controls our Logos.

The law of Karma is also referred to as the law of Cause and Effect and is basically known to us as stated in the Bible, as 'what you sow is what you will reap.' This is an important law for us to understand that makes it clear that there is a cause for every effect. Nothing happens of its own accord. There is always something or someone to make something happen. According to this law put very simply, if I hurt someone it would be presumptuous of me to think that I could get away without being penalized for my ill deed no matter how trivial. The penalty is not necessarily from the same person or at the same time nor in the same way but eventually, I will get the same energy back as I gave it out.

Karma is a learning tool of spirit, and manifests through physical circumstances. That which one places into the universe, one receives back, ten-fold. Karma does not discriminate. This is the natural principle of cause and effect. Every cause has its effect and every effect has its cause. Everything happens according to law. When we think something happens by chance it is only because we do not recognize the law. Nothing escapes the law of Karma. It is ever at work with chains of causes and effects that govern all of life and manifested matter. It has its beginning and endings in the non-material realm, the realm of spirit. It affects the rock slide that is caused by rain or wind, the snow avalanche or the throwing of dice or a card on a gambling table. The law itself is illusive and cannot be proven other than observed with the mind and is used to determine the causes and effects of any event.

When this law is used with conscious effort, desired results can be produced in a person's life by steering him or herself along definite paths of causation. When the law is used in an unconscious and haphazard mind, the effects could become potentially disastrous for the individual or group of individuals. Many so called 'accidents' could occur without warning to individuals who toil through life without awareness.

We are responsible for the very thoughts we produce and the final result for our own mental alchemy. Fear is one of the most dangerous mental causes that prevents a person from thinking and acting as the 'Higher Self' would prefer. The cause of fear is the result of a lack of knowledge about the unknown God that would be the most important educational journey in a person's life. The causes of fear can only be removed through knowledge, wisdom and understanding of universal laws. The greatest evil under the sun according to Hermes/Thoth, is not knowing God. In every minute thought, action and deed that is performed, a person sets into motion unseen chains of causes and effects which will vibrate from the mental plane throughout the entire cellular structure of the body, into the environment, and finally into the Cosmos. Eventually the vibratory energy returns to its originator upon the return swing of the pendulum.

This law is mechanically or mathematically operative and men and women of divine wisdom can scientifically manipulate its workings. The karmic law requires that every human wish finds ultimate fulfillment. Therefore, desire is the chain that binds man to the re-incarnation wheel. Karma is attracted only where the magnet of the personal ego still exists. An understanding of karma and the law of Justice underlying life's inequalities serves to free the human mind from resentment against God and man. The law of Karma is that law wherein entities arrange within themselves, on any level, to make just payment for any action committed that affects the welfare of oneself or another. The law of Karma is irrevocable and may be depended upon to bring those who stray from the law of Unity back into balance through the divine justice of the universe.

The law of Cause and Effect encompasses several sub-laws. For example like begets like. You cannot get a pear out of an orange tree. This law determines what you get according to what you do or give. If you project hate you get hate in return. If you project love you get love in return. The law works both ways for negative and positive thoughts, feelings and actions. The universe gives you back what you project to the universe. What we send forth into the universe comes back to us. We reap positive rewards for our good deeds and negative consequences of our misdeeds. Ancient scriptures state: *"All that we are is the result of what we have thought, it is founded on thought, it is made up of our thoughts. If a man acts or speaks with evil thoughts, pain follows him as the wheel follows the foot of the ox that draws the chariot."*

The Law of Knowledge

This law concerns the fact that all knowledge concerns energy, its application, and its right use or misuse. Much esoteric information is withheld until one is a disciple, and still more until one is a pledged initiate. Information is not as necessary to the training of the disciple or initiate as is the proper use of thought energy, which is full mindfulness. Knowledge is the right apprehension of the laws of energy, of the conservation of force, of the sources of energy, of its qualities, its types and its vibrations. Knowledge should be understood not only formally but in its entire multiformity.

Certain aspects of knowledge are esoteric and other aspects are exoteric. Some knowledge deals with the subjective side of life and the other type of knowledge is concerned with energy and force and with that which is being energized. We are told that the goal of evolution is for mankind to acquire full consciousness on all planes and the human race in general has so far only the physical plane somewhat under control. Information and knowledge of the life evolving through the physical forms is considered therefore esoteric knowledge as also the laws governing energy on the astral and mental planes are. Exoteric knowledge is all that can be acquired by instinct and by the use of the concrete or lower mind functioning through the physical brain. As one evolves and activates the higher abstract mind and intuition, and as certain centers in the head begin to function more esoteric knowledge will be acquired. The point that is emphasized here is the fact that all 'Knowers' must endeavor to attract others who are ready for expansion of consciousness to join the group soul on the upward arc of evolution.

There are risks involved in having too much knowledge because too much knowledge brings responsibility and power. When one uses knowledge wisely, is discrete, reserved and is able to discriminate, one increases one's capacity to receive the hidden wisdom. See also the law of Initiation.

The Law of Least Effort

Nature's intelligence functions carefree with effortless ease, with harmony and love. When we harness the forces of harmony, joy and love we create success and good fortune with effortless ease. This we do by practicing acceptance. Accept people, situations, circumstances and events as they occur. Know that this moment is as it should be because the whole universe is as it should be. To struggle against this moment is to struggle against the whole universe. Accept things as they are and not as you wish they were. Once you have accepted learn to take responsibility for situations and events that you perceive as being problems. Taking responsibility means not blaming anyone or anything. Recognize that every problem is an opportunity in disguise allowing you to transform into a greater benefit. Give up the need to defend your point of view. Remain open to all points of view and not be rigidly attached to any one of them.

There is a wonderful word in the German language that illustrates someone who acts as explained above, acting with least effort, it is to be 'gelassen.' I guess the nearest English equivalent is to be relaxed, 'cool.' To be 'cool' is to be easy about things in general i.e. not fighting or arguing, criticizing or insisting on one's own point of view. Most of us know people like that, people who just seem to float through life winning all the way effortlessly. I guess this law demonstrates why it is so. Whether they are aware of it or not they are quite obviously flowing in harmony with the energies of this law.

The Law of Leverage

This awareness indicates the future is never fixed. The future depends on what is occurring in the present, and a change in consciousness at present will effect a change in future experiences. This is related to the law of Leverage wherein a small amount of energy exerted to change the course of events at a present time (at the right moment) can move mountains in the future. This law reiterates the importance of the awareness of living in the moment.

The Law of Liability

The law of Liability states that one is held liable for the use or abuse of whatever rights one has, and one is held liable for using or neglecting to use those rights. Even where it is clearly one person's fault, the action of making that person a scapegoat for misdeeds is seldom in itself a proper solution. For the main reason for finding the cause of a mishap is to be able to prevent the mishap from recurring.

The Law of Liberation

This law is activated through right thinking to correct an undesirable situation leading to the right attitude. For example disease is a fact in nature. When this is accepted, one begins to work with the law of Liberation, with right thought, leading to right attitude and orientation and with the principle of nonresistance.

Of this nonresistance, the overpowering willingness to die, which is so frequently a characteristic of the final stage immediately preceding death is the lowest manifestation. It is nonresistance that psychologically governs coma.

This is generally recognized today in the medical field. It is the will power of the patient to overcome a disease and in worst cases a coma, to accelerate the path of recovery. It is known that if the patient has given up all hope for recovery and wishes to die then help is useless. This is the act of nonresistance and goes against this law of liberation. This is the case also with some cases of cancer. It has been known that through change of attitude and positive thinking one can heal oneself in the early stages of the disease.

The Law of Life

In accordance with the law of Life the spiritual and the psychic coordinate and balance one another in the world of the spirit and material. On this plane the soul must serve time until perfection is achieved before returning back to the Source. In accordance with this law one changes and grows constantly with each additional impression and experience of life. Issues in life are not determined by outward conditions but by one's own consciousness. The law of Life on earth requires that we human kind must acknowledge and give credit where its due namely to our Creator. We must feel gratitude and only then can we lift ourselves out of the world of limitations where we have put ourselves in of our own free will.

This law requires us to understand that the human body as it is has no power and no intelligence in its actions. We need to recognize that there is a Spirit guiding our thoughts, movements, actions, behavior and so on. The 'I,' the Spirit determines everything we do and our physical body follows this guidance. The Creator gave us consciousness and it is this consciousness that is the creative sustaining and maintaining principle. We are given dominion through our consciousness. Life is the intelligent direction within. Think of your body as your radio, and your consciousness is the director of your radio. You can tune into or out of any activity or condition as you wish. You can change the program of your life if you do not like it and make it better. The law of Life says that the only way to expand is to give of one's self. The more you give of yourself the more you and your world will expand. Life is the greatest of all mysteries. The truth of life is to be found in respiration, in breathing. See the law of Respiration. See also the law of Synthesis.

The Law of Light

Cosmic Light = Spirit = God = All that is.

Light cannot be perceived without darkness, see also the law of Balance. However, light being of the highest vibration always prevails. Light is absolute. Enlightenment is an outcome of light. First we need to realize that everywhere about us there exists a universal substance which we call Cosmic Light. The Bible refers to this as Spirit. This is the One Pure Primal Essence—out of which emanates all Creation. It is the 'Pure Life Substance,' of the First Cause, God. This is Infinite and we may draw upon it at any time, for anything that we require, by the power of concentration. This 'Pure Electronic Light' is the great limitless storehouse of the Universe. In it is all perfection and out of it comes all that is.

We are presently witnessing the Earth as it is passing through the throes of a tremendous new birth, and will be in a transition period in the few years ahead. It is changing now in a Cosmic Way, from the attitude of war into that of peace, in accordance with the new age of Aquarius. We will witness changes such as hatred to love, selfishness to unselfishness and into full recognition that in the future, we the human family must exert strength enough to live according to the law of Love.

We have arrived at a certain time in the process of evolution of our planet and we humanity must express the full peace, harmony, perfection and the divine plan of the system to which we belong. When the time comes we humanity either move froward in fulfillment of God's plan or those of us who will not

Flowing with Universal Laws

come into alignment with the new vibrations, will move on to another school room of the Universe, until those personalities learn obedience to life. The law of Life is heaven, peace, harmony and love to every created thing. Even the ethers of infinite space express this harmony everywhere. We human beings are the only creators of hell. Each one of us carries our own heaven or hell with us every moment of our life, for these are but the results of our own mental and emotional states, which we have created because of our own attitude. All misery, darkness and ignorance exist only because of lack of love. The Light does not receive disharmony into itself. As the student enters the light he becomes all light hence all perfection. To have disharmony drop away from one's body or one's affairs, one must let go of all thought, feeling, and words about imperfection. It is forgiveness that fills all with Lights Perfection.

The Law of Love

Love is the key to everything, building and disintegrating of forms and gives the urge to progress. The law of Love is one of the seven laws of the solar system and is the law of the astral plane, the plane of emotions. This law aims at the transmutation of the desire nature and links it up with the greater magnetism of the love aspect on the Buddhic plane. On the astral plane, the home of our desires, originate the feelings which we call personal love, in its lowest form, it shows itself as animal passion. In the highest form it manifests as pure love. We are unfailingly responsible to act with love in every thought, word, deed, intent, motive and action.

The stages of love in the personality develops with a simple and selfish love for the self, then expands to love of family and friends, and more people until it arrives at the stage of group love consciousness which is the characteristic of the soul. At this level one is a master of compassion, loves, suffers with and is loyal to his kind. This love gradually develops from love for humanity to love of the universe and all forms of divine manifestation. The first love in the personality is love for the three worlds, the second love in the soul is for the solar system and the third, which is love of the Monad, demonstrates Cosmic Love. Love was the primary motive for manifestation, love bears all on the path of return and love eventually perfects all.

When one is aware of divine love as more than just an abstract principle, then one will realize that one can generate it at will, and direct it consciously, to accomplish whatever one decrees. Divine love for the Ascended Masters is a Presence, an Intelligence, a Principle of Light, a Power, an Activity, and a Substance. Love is magic. When we refer to that great Love of Life it is the Scepter of Power. It is the law of all that is perfect. It is the illumining power of all wisdom, and it is energy without limit to produce whatever manifestation we command to appear in action. We are required to live our life with love. Love is the key and the motor to life. When you live your life with love you cannot go wrong. The three expressions of love are, love in the personality, love in the Soul, and love in the Monad.

Love has the highest frequency vibration and is the best cure for healing. The feeling of love produces certain chemical reactions as well as hormonal effects in the body that create an emotional high unmatched by any other means of healing. Only the few realize that you need not depend on anyone or anything else to experience the feeling of love. You can develop love from within you for yourself and for all life.

The Law of Lotus

This is the name given to the influence from the cosmic law of Attraction that linked the two poles of spirit and matter producing upon the plane of mind the egoic lotus or the 'Flower of the Self.' It is the law that enables the lotus to draw from the lower water and matter aspect the moisture and heat needed for its unfoldment. It governs the process of petal unfoldment and therefore, itself demonstrates as a triple law:

The law of Solar Heat - Knowledge petals.
The law of Solar Light - Love petals
The law of Solar Fire - Sacrifice petals

There are several energy centers distributed all over the human body through which the human connects with the universe. These energy centers are known as chakras. Chakra is Sanskrit for the 'Wheel of Life.' As the human develops in consciousness the chakras unfold. The symbol for each chakra is a lotus with a certain number of petals. As the individual progresses on the path of evolution each chakra opens and flows and the lotus of knowledge unfolds its petals. All of this occurs on the psychic level. The symbol of the root chakra is a four petal lotus and for the hip chakra a six petal lotus. The solar plexus is represented by a ten petal lotus. A twelve petal lotus is the symbol for the heart chakra and a sixteen petal lotus for the throat chakra. For the third eye chakra the lotus symbol has ninety six petals and for the crown chakra on top of the head it is a thousand petal lotus. As the individual expands in consciousness the lotus petals open to allow universal energies to flow through the human. When all petals are open then the individual has reached divinity.

Margo Kirtikar Ph.D.

The Law of Macrocosm and Microcosm

The law of Macrocosm and Microcosm is the first Law of Infinity. This law indicates that the whole is equal, more or less to the sum of its parts, depending on the ordering of those parts. In each living thing, in everything that exists there is within it some part of the whole. The whole is the grouping together of each of its parts in a certain order. An analogy is the sea or ocean in comparison with a drop of dew on the petal of a flower.

The Law of Magic

The law of magic is the law that creates change. Physical change comes about through the change of consciousness. Consciousness changes in response to anticipation. Anticipation results from imagery and preparation, fears and desires based on fallacies or facts. Preparation for change, changes consciousness, which results in physical change. The quality and quantity of description and imagery, the intensity and consistency of attitudes and actions, the collective or disruptive energies of others, all work together to influence the direction and course of the change. Every one to some degree, for good or ill, is both victim and master of the law of Magic. The law of Magic is an extension of the law of Unity. See also the law of Miracles.

The Law of Magnetic Control

This law is one of the seven laws of our solar system under the three major laws. It is through this law that the spiritual nature of the human governs the personality through the soul nature. This is the law on the Buddhic plane. It is the law of Love that holds all together and that draws all upward. It is also a demonstration of the law of Attraction. It is this law that holds the atoms together. It is the law where sex expression as we know it is transmuted and elevated. This holds predominantly on the Buddhic plane, and in the development of the control of this, lies hid the control of the personality by the Monad via the egoic body.

A second description on a very physical level, is that every thought we have creates a match that comes back to us like a boomerang. This law teaches us to control or every thought, for example if we think of doing harm to someone else, we are doing harm unto ourselves as the energy colored by the quality of our wicked thought will eventually come back to haunt us.

The Law of Magnetic Impulse

Also known as the first step towards marriage or the law of the polar union. It results in an eventual union between the man or atom and the group that produces harmonious group relations. It is also known as the law of the polar union, and the symbol is two fiery balls united by a triangle of fire, this picturing the triple interplay between all atomic structures.

The Law of Magnetism

This law produces the unifying of the personality, the physical, the emotional and the mental bodies and is of a much higher order than the law of physical sex. The forces here are not concerned with the lower aspect of physical sex. This law is concerned with the body of the human in the final three stages of the path of evolution. The stage of high intellectual or artistic attainment, the stage of discipleship, and the stage of threading the path of return, i.e. The fifth, sixth and seventh stages in the evolution of the human being.

The Law of Manifestation

The law of Divine Manifestation requires one to believe in the principle that whatever is needed for one's growth and fruition will be supplied by the Universe, for whatever price one truly believes is fair. But one must believe he or she truly has the right to receive the manifestation at the price of energy cost the entity believes is fair. If it is a worthy request, and one believes it is allotted at the time of asking, it will come. A worthy request expressed through prayer, imaging, ritual or whatever method, is anything that harms no one, but benefits all involved. It is a win-win relationship. Anything that harms another, either in the process or the outcome of manifestation, is not of the Divine and will carry a karmic debt. The spirit is manifested in the flesh. Only through this manifestation can one come to know oneself.

Spirit manifests its thoughts through the readiness and willingness of its soul. Souls manifest their thoughts through the readiness and willingness of their intentions. Manifestation of the spiritual leads to manifestation in the physical. Only thought exists, therefore, it is important to know that everything which exists on the physical plane is a result of pure thought.

Decide what you want, state it as clearly as possible in every minute detail, let it go and assume that it is already done. Do not doubt. It is usually our internal sabotage patterns, disbelief and doubt that stop manifestation of our innermost dreams and desires. When we are in alignment with the Divine Will, our ability to manifest is guaranteed provided we have unwavering faith.

The Law of Mantras

In accordance with this law there exists a secret knowledge that is based on the study of sounds and of the differences of vibration levels. These sounds and vibrations vary in accordance with the state of consciousness of each human being and all life on earth. The basic sounds which have the power of establishing communication with the spiritual world are known as mantras. Mantras are the most powerful media to free the practices from illusion or ignorance. From the explosion caused by the training of Mantras, extremely small power waves or vibrations result that take the practicer to his goal. Through the Mantra itself, a practicer, mingles his own existence with the eternal power. There are three types of Mantra reciting: Verbal recitation, Recitation in low voice, and recitation of Mantra without voice or mental recitation.

Each mantra is a combination of sounds and words and is a linkage to a certain aspect of the absolute, a certain manifestation of Divinity. In true mantra practice, one forgets the fact that the self is chanting, becomes the mantra itself, and attains the state where nothing but the mantra exists. One's being then connects with the Higher Being. The mantra connects with the Higher Being if it is the name of a Master, or connects with the Ray of Light emanating from God, if it is a sound-AUM, OM, HU, ALLELUJAH, ALLAH, etc. The practice of chanting mantras is profoundly beneficial in raising the vibration of self. Sound like color has a powerful affect on the human system. The wrong mantras or sounds can be detrimental. A combination of certain sounds can at a lower level of consciousness, put one in relation with the corresponding forces to obtain certain powers. There are mantras that can kill and mantras that can heal. This kind of magic is achieved by consciously manipulating the lower vibrations. There is also a higher magic that deals with vibrations on a higher plane of consciousness. This can be words, poetry or music. On this level the mantra serves to connect with one higher force or being.

In ancient days this art was well known as wizards and witches used such mantras constantly to create miracles good or evil. This method is still used today by those who have this secret knowledge.

The Law of Meditation

This law is defined as a current of unified thought. It is a continuum of mental effort to assimilate the object of meditation, free from any other effort to assimilate other objects. When meditating on God, the most profound happening will bring a merging of the two, the personality and the divine within, or 'enlightenment' as Buddhist call this occurrence. The very least that may happen is the calming of self. Technically speaking, meditation is the process where the head center is awakened and is brought under control and used. When this happens, the soul and the personality are coordinated and fused, and 'oneness with the divine' is experienced. This experience produces in the human a tremendous inflow of spiritual energy, galvanizing the whole being into activity and bringing to the surface not only the dormant good, but also the evil.

The Creator has built in special instruments in the human body for man to develop in order to receive and transmit certain cosmic energies. Through meditation we can develop these organs and the inner strength so that we can receive and transmit the sound waves from the cosmos, which are of a much higher vibration level, without suffering any damage to our body. These built in instruments are found in the chakras, the solar plexus and in certain centers in the brain for example the pineal gland and the pituitary gland commonly referred to as the third eye. Without them we are incapable of receiving or understanding the cosmic signals that are constantly arriving from the universe. As a person meditates regularly and begins to receive the cosmic waves, something inside develops which enables one to stand up to the greater tension. This stage cannot be achieved in a hurry nor can it be forced by artificial methods. It needs patience and regularity and constant meditation until the organism has a chance to grow gradually stronger and is able to stand up to the strains as cosmic energies are received.

When one is advanced enough one can with concentration and an intensive thought, reach someone across the world anywhere by just thinking about them. This is to us known as telepathy. One is just as easily able to obtain any element from the universe, minerals for example if one's body needs that instead of actually taking tablets. One can also acquire any quality that one desires from any entity, as an example, an artist concentrates on a great long gone favorite artist and calls forth those qualities from the universe. Distance makes no difference and you don't even have to know the whereabouts. All this is possible, however, it is not as easy as it sounds. It requires many years of diligent practice, the development of the higher mind and abstract thought, and above all the spiritual faculties. This can only be developed over several life times. Through reincarnation, all work physical and spiritual that is done and whatever faculties are developed during any one life time, are carried over to the next life span.

Meditation involves the living of a one-pointed life at all times every day. When meditation is carried out systematically with years of effort, supplemented by meditative living and at one-pointed service, this will eventually arouse the entire system and bring the lower man under the influence and control of the spiritual man. It will awaken the centers in the etheric body through the chakras and stimulate the kundalini fire, that mysterious stream of energy that lies dormant at the

Flowing with Universal Laws

base of the spine. When this process is carried out with care and under direction over a long period of time, the awakening will take place normally and under the law of Being itself. See the law of Reincarnation, the law of Prayer and Meditation, the law of Telepathy and the law of Being.

The Law of Meekness

'Blessed be the meek' may seem literally to support those kindly timid souls who are an easy prey for the more aggressive souls. What it refers to, however, is to the one who is able to follow the law of Non Resistance to the point of inheriting the earth and all things thereof. To be meek does not mean to be an easy mark nor to be a doormat for anyone to walk over nor does it mean to be submissive to the conditions of discord and disorder. We are meek only to the natural laws of the universe. Meekness is, therefore, strength acquired when we do not argue, when we do not become proud and boastful, when we do not insist on being right in any argument. Meekness is the steel of one's nature and is enduring. Meekness is the strength by which we win an argument in refusing to argue. The spirit of meekness is recognized as being cooperative, persistent application, accurate computation and perfect harmony. See also the law of Non Resistance.

The Law of Mentalism

This law gives us the opportunity to learn from our mistakes and successes. I believe that we can learn more from our mistakes which are usually painful experiences and the next time we will usually make changes to correct that particular situation, then we learn from our successes. This would need us to take the time to reflect on ourselves, our life, all our mistakes and all our accomplishments.

The Law of Mercy

The law of Mercy is that law which allows us to forgive all error; to forgive equally those who err against us as we err against them. This law requires us to be merciful. To be merciful is akin to the law of Love, and if one obeys the law of Mercy there can be no error in the world.

The Law of Miracles

Life is a miracle, and we all create miracles every day. This law can be activated by any person who has realized that the 'Essence' of creation is 'Light.' A master is able to employ his or her divine knowledge of light phenomena to project instantly into perceptible manifestation the flawless light atoms. The actual form of the projection whatever it is, for example, water into wine, is determined by the master's wish and by his powers of will and visualization. All events in our precisely adjusted universe are lawfully wrought and lawfully explicable. The so-called miraculous powers of a great master are a natural accompaniment to his or her exact understanding of subtle laws that operate in the inner cosmos of consciousness. Nothing is a miracle except in the profound sense that everything is a miracle. Is anything more miraculous than that each of us is encased in an intricately organized body, and is set upon on earth whirling through space among the stars?

The Law of Moderation

This natural law states that anything in extreme is as harmful as insufficiency. The Indian scriptures, the Bhagavad Gita warn us to be always moderate in our approach and not to go to extremes in our pursuit of spirituality and in our search for God, as exaggeration can have negative and undesirable effects. Moderation is a greater virtue than over indulgence or total abstinence. The practice of Yoga for example is a moderation of conduct and internal adjustment. Moderation is to know when one has arrived at the point that once crossed can bring destruction. In practicality for example a cook needs to use just the right amount of salt or spices in the food, a few grains too many and the food would be inedible, too salty or too spicy to eat. An artist knows intuitively when the work at hand is complete and perfect, one stroke too many could ruin the whole artwork. One can love someone dearly but too much love can also smother and suffocate. Too many rules and regulations are confining, however, total freedom without any guidelines or limitations can lead to disaster. Moderation is to recognize that certain perfect level or point and to know when to stop. To be able to do that one has to be fully aware and to have total control over one's faculties.

The Law of Monadic Return

This law concerns the force of evolution and is the sum total of three influences. The strength of vibrations from the seven stars of the Great Bear depend upon the closeness of the connection and the accuracy of the alignment between any particular Heavenly Man and His Prototype. Second is the Seven Sisters, or the Pleiades. Third is the Sun Sirius. It is the appearance or the disappearance of these waves of life-force which sweeps into incarnation the divine pilgrims, and which brings about the cyclic manifestation of such great Lives as the 'Silent Watcher' and the 'Great Sacrifice.' Within limits, man is the controller of his destiny, wielding forces and energies, manipulating lesser lives and controlling lesser centers of energy and as time passes his radius of control becomes even more extensive.

The Law of Money

The law of Money states that money is but an artificially created symbol used as a substitute to store energies borrowed, earned, spent, owed, claimed or exchanged. To be 'good' money the symbol must be acceptable to others in a society who are willing to part with valuables or energies in exchange for the money symbol. Each society may further define its own money and the use thereof.

On a practical tone, money comes to those who love and respect money and it stays with those who use it wisely. As energy begets energy, money begets money. Some esoteric people wrongly believe that money is dirty or unimportant. Money is manifested energy or solidified spirit and should circulate widely and wisely. Hoarding money is a violation of this law as it is blocking of the circulation of energy in its solidified form.

The Law of Non-intervention

This law concerns the individual right of people and society situations to serve self rather than live in the vibration of service to others. This law prevents physical beings and non physical beings from intervening or correcting what they see as wrong or harmful. If this law is violated, there is great karma incurring. Another aspect of this law is that spirit is not permitted to channel material to a recipient that would force a change in the evolution of the person. There is exception when the channeller is willing to undergo a trance, and the consciousness leaves the body for another consciousness to enter and impart knowledge that was previously unknown to the individual.

The Law of Non-Judgement

The Universal Spirit does not judge us; judgements are human inventions, a means to compare, contrast and control as we judge ourselves against artificial and often idealistic standards of perfection, morality or truth. Under the law of Equalities, our judgements attract judgement to us in equal measure. The life karmic review conducted by your after death is a conditional living in the third dimension of duality.

Law of Non-Resistance

True harmony cannot come from inharmony, nor peace from discord. It seems contrary to the natural reaction of a body, for when we meet with opposition it seems natural to steel our energies and collect our wits, and use whatever means we have to outwit and break down the opposition. Yet as contrary as it may seem in one sense, a meek and Non-Resistant position taken is the more powerful and easier way to utilize the forces of nature. When we are working to gain success and to bring forth an increase of supply or material wealth and we sometimes get into the habit of talking and fearing hard times. We may talk about our neighbor or criticize the method he used to get ahead. We may fear business conditions and when we see the graph take a downward swing we fear for our investments and our job. When we do theses things we are acting foolishly. For such an act is resistance of thought. Thought action is just as substantial as physical action, therefore it is wise to realize, monitor, and modify our thoughts as much as we do our physical actions. Thoughts are matter and have a major effect on the flow of circumstances in our lives.

When we meet an obstacle we may stop our progress to collect forces and put up a fight to remove it. This resistance causes friction. Friction causes irritation and an inflammation. For this reason our lives becomes hard and exacting. It is like machinery that is resisted upon. The machine breaks down and wears out. It is not the movement of the machine but the friction that causes the breakdown and difficulties. Friction is opposition and resistance. If we go through life, fighting, opposing, resisting, arguing, we are bound to meet with many obstacles and likely become so occupied fighting them that we lose sight of our real goal. If we strive to make little of the obstacle and keep our minds on the objective or desire we set out to gain, we will ultimately win.

In the beginning we have many obstacles and trials to strive past. The wise one will not fight these obstacles, but bless them and go on. As we go on with faith and assurance, we grow stronger and become more momentous in our progress towards our goal. The less we resist the better opportunity we have to build a stronger momentum in our progress.

"Blessed are the Meek" may seem literally to support those kindly timid souls who are an easy prey for their more aggressive brothers. Rather, it refers to the one who is able to follow the law of Non-Resistance to the point of inheriting the earth and all things thereof. To be meek does not mean to be an easy mark nor to be a doormat for anyone to walk over. To be meek does not mean that we are submissive to the conditions of discord and disorder. We are meek only to the natural laws of the universe. Meekness is therefore strength acquired when we do not argue, when you do not become angry or boastful and proud, when you do not insist upon having your rights in a quarrelsome manner. Meekness is the steel of one's nature. It is enduring. Meekness is the strength by which you win an argument in refusing to argue. In science we recognize the spirit of meekness as cooperative, persistent application, accurate computation, perfect harmony and symmetry of design and color.

When we integrate the law of Non-Resistance into our lives, letting go of every worried thought, every fear, doubt, complaint, argument, and angry thought, we tend to shorten the time for our goal to be reached. Remove and dissolve every obstacle by blessing it and be willing to understand it. Make your obstacles as stepping stones of progress leading to your highest good.

Margo Kirtikar Ph.D.

The Law of Number Measure and Weight

It is written in the Sepher Yetzirah, the Book of Creation, one of the oldest Jewish texts that God designed, that is, engraved, carved, weighed, permuted and transformed, the 22 letters of the Hebrew Alphabet to form the foundation of his creation and how he combined these letters to generate the words by which 'He depicted all that was formed and all that would be formed.' The text states that 'God placed them in a circle.' The word circle which can also be translated as 'sphere' or 'cycle' used to denote the cycle events in the world. The Book of Creation also states that God weighed the letters which refers to the 'weight' of their numerical values. This natural metaphor is used by modern mathematicians with phrases such as 'weighted sum' and 'weighted average.' The values of each letter may be seen in the Jewish Alphabet Table. Aleph (A) is the lightest having a weight of Unity and Tav (T) the cross, is the heaviest with a weight of 400 in number. The primary significance of many alphanumeric relations is often immediately obvious, as with identities such as Wheel which equals the number 66 and Alpha Omega which equals 801 The Creator. A proper understanding is required with a great deal of study, experience and patience with heavy emphasis on virtue and respect. The alphanumeric relations encode the deepest mysteries of life.

The Law of One

All that is exists is part of God Oneness. This awareness indicates all is one and all reside within the law of One. All souls are cells of the body of this awareness, and when awareness of the law of One is present, one has no need to struggle or to compete, as one would be fighting with oneself within one body. All who understand this law of One realize that all that appears to be separate is an illusion. There is only One Power in existence, only One Creator and One God. Nothing exists outside of the Creator. 'I' and 'me' do not exist only 'we' and 'us.' Even we and us are temporary perceptions as all that is, is ONE. Separation from God exists only as a misperception and therefore does not exist at all. Perhaps we will witness a time in the future when awareness of the meaning of this law will grow. When educators can teach this law to children at a young age we will see a new generation of peace loving people grow.

The Law of Opportunity

Under this law opportunities or choices are unlimited and always lead to success. That which is needed is available when needed. What is mandatory is that we recognize and act as the opportunity presents itself to us. As it says in the Bible 'Ask and it shall be given unto you.' And 'Knock and it shall be opened unto you.' You have got to take the initiative and move to act. Opportunities and choices are presented to us daily according to our needs, it is up to us to be aware and to see these for what they are and to make our choices. Many opportunities in life are lost because one is either too blind to see them or too afraid to take action.

The Law of Order and Creation

That which is destined to be appears in Divine Order. Any attempt to place anything out of order is a violation of the universal law of Balance. Confusion does not exist. Divine Plan always enfolds in a precise and predetermined manner. The beginning of law carried all the way through. And that which comes or begins first is conceived in spirit, grows in the mental and manifests in the material.

The Law of Paradox

The law of Paradox is the law that recognizes the movement of energies in four dimensions simultaneously. This awareness indicates the law of Paradox as that which combines the law of Cause and Effect along with the law of Inertia, the law of Microcosm and Macrocosm, and the law of Vibration. This awareness indicates that the law of Paradox relates to that which is the focus of attention. Whereby energies do come together in a collision at a certain point and whereby that point does create a relationship using the law of Relativity as a type of, as a part of itself. Whereby this point in relationship does reflect that which is the microcosms and macrocosm, does relate to movements which are occurring at a certain momentum. This as the law of Inertia whereby an equal and opposite reaction does occur which moves entities into another dimension on this macrocosmic level and on those vibrations in between. This relating to the echoing effect of an action.

The law of Paradox when seen in a flat plane, would be likened unto a stone dropped in a stream, and watching the ripples move out. The law of Paradox seen in a cube of space would create vibrations in all directions, whereby that stone was emanating an energy, though not being dripped, but simply vibration, and that energy would be felt in various places within that cube of space. When the law is in the fourth dimensional level as that which occurs in all places simultaneously on certain vibratory rates likened unto the ringing of a bell that vibrates every particle of energy within its periphery. The law of Paradox touches into such high levels of vibration and such dense levels of vibration simultaneously that the entire area appears to be alive, and whatever is said about one level can also hold true about the next, yet can also appear to be untrue.

All spiritual answers are found in the opposite perception than that which manifests in the physical. In other words, this material world is all about 'control' the Spiritual world answer in comparison is about 'surrender.' To be near the Divine we need to give up control e.g. to sacrifice the ego and to surrender to the Divine in us. Sacrificing the ego does not mean to give up the ego or to kill it. A well developed ego is mandatory but the ego must recognize at some point Divinity and be willing to surrender.

The Law of Patience

The law of Patience states that all things must have their time and their season whereby they may work their action to proper fruition. Patience involves spiritual, mental and physical thought and action. Through this law we get to know our self, to test and measure our ideals, to have faith and to seek understanding through all the other virtues. Patience allows all other virtues to manifest more profoundly. Patiently we realize that any fault we see in another is one we have personal knowledge of from prior experience. Patiently we seek true understanding, not just knowledge, as we realize that every soul is totally unique and will come to its enlightenment in its own time. Patience is a virtue and is a quality of the soul.

The Law of Patterns

This law states that any pattern or habit, whether it is good or bad, tends to reassert itself over time, unless we break the pattern by doing something different. If we have a good habit we can reinforce the pattern with small self rewards. We have the power of spontaneous action and the power of the imagination to do old things in new ways to change and to restructure our life and our behavior pattern. Some of our change ability is influenced by the ways we have learned in our youth and through conditioning. We learned to make sense of the world by observing patterns in order to survive. When we find the patterns disfunctional or destructive, however, this law allows us to do something different that will give sufficient impact to interrupt the old pattern and replace it with a new and better one.

Most of us tend to be slaves of our habits. With self awareness we can reassess our habits periodically and we can make the effort to change them, when we find them to be detrimental to our well being and growth.

Margo Kirtikar Ph.D.

The Law of Peace

The law of Peace states that peace comes from within, and is related to the concept of surrender. But peaceful surrender cannot be to that which is divisive and polarized or greater conflict will follow. Under this law we are warned that any compromise with forces that divide instead of unify, that oppress instead of liberate, that harm instead of benefit, will inevitably lead to greater conflict. This law allows surrender only to that which brings a total unity by reconciling the yes and no and other oppositions.

Peace is not only found in harmony, but may also be found in conflict when that conflict is essential for the harmony, welfare and liberty of everyone involved. It also suggests that inner peace nourishes external harmony, and grows by increments and degrees even as yes and no are merged into a maybe, even as you and I are brought together into we. With inner peace, one can witness harmony even in the midst of conflict. Through this law of Peace a soft response will often put a wrathful tongue to rest. It is through the maintenance of an inner state of peace and harmony that initiates allow all others their unique truth and their unique creation upon the earth plane. Acceptance of all that is means that one must embrace the dance and rhythm of earth as it currently is, unconditionally, even though it is full of pain, fear, judgement and deficiency. Unconditional acceptance does not mean that an initiate must partake in the dance of pain, fear, judgement or deficiency but that they must allow others to dance in such a way if they choose to do so. 'Being in the world but not of it' is

Flowing with Universal Laws

only accomplished as one separates their thought form from mass conscious experiences. In order to retain an inner state of peace, harmony and centeredness, our channels have learned not to listen to the news or any form of media including the radio. They also do not read the newspapers or magazines nor do they maintain contact with those who perpetuate abusive or judgmental patterns. To embody a state of harmlessness, initiates must take full conscious responsibility for every thought and every action that they participate in.

The Law of Penetration

The law of Penetration states that anything which is looked at with great attention with a great quality of consciousness penetrates directly to the heart, and then emanates into all of consciousness. This awareness suggests that when a healing is given to someone, that the healer also gives the suggestion. This awareness indicates this in particular to these who find it difficult to accept a healing for any particular length of time or a permanent healing. Another awareness also suggests that when a healer gives you a healing and states that this healing appears to be good for an 'x' number of months, or more, then other forces within your own psyche are capable of taking over and to continue with the healing process for the stated time. This is connected with the law of Suggestion.

The Law of Perception

Perception reveals perception e.g. we see things not as they are, but as we are according to our perceptions of our experiences of life. Each Soul's ability to discern highest truth is in direct proportion to its initiative to achieve it. Our thoughts, ideas, desires differ as much as we differ in our looks from each other. If ten people look at the same scene or hear the same story, they will give ten different perceptions. How we see and hear and perceive depends on the conditioning that we have had, from what we have experienced in our lives, past and present.

The Law of Perfection

This law concerns the absolute perfection of the process of our unfolding. From a transcendental perspective, everyone and everything is unconditionally perfect. From a conventional viewpoint, perfection does not exist. Excellence is the best we can achieve and achieving takes time and practice. When we understand the larger picture, we understand our role and responsibility in helping the world we live in to become a more loving, giving, kinder and gentler. When we live up to this responsibility, we expand into the perfection of our higher selves. Spirit is perfect. Consciousness is perfect. Perfection is an absolute. Perfection, like truth, has many aspects, but also like truth, is the highest vibration. Nothing exists which is not perfect.

The Law of Periodicity

Training for the aspirant will be cyclic and will have its ebb and flow, as everything else in nature. Times of activity succeed times of 'pralaya' or rest, and periods of registered contact alternate with periods of apparent silence. If the 'student' develops as desired, each paralayic period is succeeded by one of greater activities and of more potent achievement. Rhythm, ebb and flow, and the measured beat of the pulsating life are ever the law of the Universe. In learning to respond to the vibration of the high places, this rhythmic periodicity must be borne in the mind.

The Law of Permanence

An entity attains permanence when it remains integrated without the vessel that holds it. The soul within the form.

The Law of Perspective

This law means determining what is more important to you and what will produce Soul growth. Activating this law starts with some deep reflection. What is life to you? Why do you approach it? What produces the greatest satisfaction and security for you? If you would die tomorrow what would you want to have accomplished and produced with your life? With these question in mind, you can begin to decide what to do first. What desires will you need to accomplish first, second, third and so on. This is a very important law because you can fulfill many desires in your life only when you put them in order. Without order, you become scattered and unfocused. With proper perspective you can learn planning and you can also learn to use you time and energy most efficiently.

Margo Kirtikar Ph.D.

The Law of Planetary Affinity

This law is in connection with the interaction of the planets with each other and their eventual union. The term planetary affinity is used in the occult teaching specifically in connection with the interaction of the planets with each other and their eventual unity. As we know, the planetary schemes, the seven sacred planets, will eventually synthesize, or absorb the life of the planets which are not termed sacred and the numerous planetoids, as far as the four kingdom of nature are concerned. The absorption of the spirit aspect proceeds under the law of Synthesis. The four minor planetary schemes become first the two, and then the one. This process is repeated until the final one is eventually merged in the sun, producing one flaming ball of fire.

The seven sacred planets are the Vulcan, Mercury, Venus, Jupiter, Saturn, Neptune, Uranus. Mars, Earth, Pluto, the Moon veiling a hidden planet, and the Sun also veiling a planet are considered in the occult science as non sacred planets. Some understanding is here necessary as to the relation between the human being and the planets. The seven major force centers, known as chakras, in the etheric body are the distributing agencies and electrical batteries that provide the dynamic force and energy to the human, they produce definite effects upon her/his outer physical manifestation. Through this constant activity the qualities of the human appear, the ray tendencies appear and the point of progress on the ladder of evolution is thus clearly indicated. The planetary influences completely condition and control the unevolved human being with no soul experience. The moment that one becomes aware of one's own soul and begins to control one's own path in life, the influences of the planets begin to weaken gradually. One begins to gain control over the forces flowing through one and one becomes receptive to the subtler and higher energies of the solar system and the twelve governing constellations.

When soul and body, consciousness and form are blended then the disciple brings about this relationship within one's little system and the planetary Logos on a far larger scale within one's range of influence and control. This blending or fusion produces Transfiguration, the third initiation. In this process one carries all the four kingdoms in nature. Mineral, Plant, animal and human. The five non sacred planets correspond to the system of the human being: the first is the physical outer shell the body, the etheric or vital body, the astral body and the mental body plus a fusion of all four to make the fifth which is the personality. The conscious individual. The four kingdoms in nature plus the Kingdom of God.

The Law of Planning

Planning is a function of divine intelligence nothing happens by accident in God's universe. Planning is mandatory. Even failure to plan is temporary and is a function of the divine plan.

The Law of Polarity

For everything there is an opposite which is equal. Everything is dual. Like and unlike are the same. Opposites are identical in nature but different in degree. All paradoxes may be reconciled. The evidence of this principle is observed in the polarity of planets and the various celestial bodies that includes our earth, solar system and galaxy. Without the law of polarity light, gravity and electricity would not be possible. On the mental plane, this principle manifests itself in the heart center of each person as the enlightened or the dark mind. The principle of polarity make possible the choices we make on the scale of life between good and evil, right and wrong, generosity and greed, love and fear, truth and lies. The law of cause and effect is closely connected to polarity and holds us true to the choices and actions we make by returning to us what we have measured out to others. Like the swing of the pendulum, it always returns where it began. 'Do unto others, as you would have them to you.' This principle establishes the paradox or the dual aspects of reality. 'Everything that is, has its double.' Positive and negative, light and darkness, hot and cold, love and fear, morality and immorality all are two extremes of the same pole.

Margo Kirtikar Ph.D.

The Law of Poverty

The law of Poverty states that to the degree one withholds one's productivity and energy in hopes someone else will offer theirs instead, to that same degree, an entity earns and experiences poverty. When you take you become poorer. When you give you become richer because giving triggers stagnant forces, imbedded in one's being and as soon as one shares with others these forces begin to flow abundantly, making you richer. Poverty does not refer to monetary poverty only but also to physical, emotional, mental and spiritual. We experienced for example in the last century a poverty of spirituality in the western hemisphere. So if you have a wealth of money, health, love or talent and you do not share this with fellow humans, to inspire them, to spread joy around you, you inevitably experience poverty of the spirit.

The Law of Practice

We are all familiar with this law. Practice makes perfect. To become proficient in any field we need to practice. There is no accomplishment of any goal without practice. The more intelligent the practice is the greater the proficiency and the sooner the goal is attained. This holds true for absolutely everything, whether it is learning a language or learning to sing or dance. It is the same if we want to learn to swim, skate or fly, cook or drive a car. The more we practice the better we get. Intelligent practice is the secret of attainment.

The Law of Praise

This law is connected with the law of Increase. Praise is faith in action, without faith you have nothing to build upon. When you energize your desires with faith and praise you work within universal laws and the power of the mind is used properly and efficiently. Learn to render praise, and always to be thankful for the good at hand. 'As you sow, so shall you reap' is a basic, organic law which works in nature. Equally important is the fact that this law applies in our lives as well as in nature. You sow the seeds by spoken words, by acts towards others, and by the very thoughts you hold in your mind. What happens in your life is the fruit springing from those seeds. In other words, you yourself sow the seeds of your own experience. The law does not judge what you should or should not do. The law will reproduce exactly as you sow. Once you have planted a good seed, like a farmer, you wait. Do not dig it up to see if it is growing. Be patient with the law, it always works. Praise the creator in all things, good and bad. Giving praise to divinity exalts us.

Praise is an avenue of prayer and desire through which the spiritual law expresses itself. When you offer praise you lift the consciousness to a higher realm and become a greater channel to receive the good that is ever waiting to come to you. Praise opens a little door in your mind that enables you to draw closer to the universe and to be attuned to the Divine forces within and about you. Praise expands and opens the mind upward, while it's opposite, condemnation, contracts and restricts. You have noticed how a child responds to praise, with a glow and gladness. As does the universe, reflecting joy and rejoicing at the act of praise. When we sing and praise in the face of adversity, the adversity will soon disappear. This is not a promise or idle talk. This is a universal law.

Margo Kirtikar Ph.D.

The Law of Prayer and Meditation

Prayer is a conscious concrete effort to communicate with the Consciousness of Life and its Creator and so we speak to God. Prayer is also an aligning, cleansing process opening up our inner selves to the Source of all life and demonstrating that we are anxious for enlightenment and guidance. In prayer we speak to God, to the Higher Power, but more often than not, unfortunately, we do not wait long enough to hear a reply. Prayer is the forerunner to meditation.

Meditation is the freeing and emptying of ourselves of obstacles that hinder communication and allow us to channel the Life Force, spiritually, mentally and physically. Meditation is the attunement of our physical, emotional and mental bodies to the spiritual source. In meditation correctly aligned and unobstructed, the creative forces of God can rise along both the spiritual and physical channels in our bodies, and are disseminated through our sensitive spiritual chakras. In meditation we can meet the Divine within the temple of our own body.

It is only through the practice of meditation that one can get to know oneself, to gain control of the self, to develop virtues and spiritual qualities. There are certain conditions that have to be met before one can begin to meditate. One must be inwardly calm and free which means, the mind must be free of all mundane daily occupation. Certain preparations are also necessary, for example allocating a certain place and a specific time for the meditation. Lighting incense or a candle helps to cleanse and to focus the energy to make it easier for you to

Flowing with Universal Laws

relax in preparation. It helps when this meditation corner, if possible at all, is reserved specifically for the purpose of meditation so that energies remain pure and accumulate to enhance the meditation process.

Preparing yourself for meditation you relax and free yourself in body mind and emotions until you have achieved the feeling of having escaped from the prison of everyday life. As you free yourself in time you begin to feel something inside you growing, expanding and the divine flow rising within you. When you have felt this you will begin to be convinced that the soul is a reality, that the divine world exists and countless creatures inhabit this world. When you can achieve this stage then you begin to feel your faculties obeying you. It feels as if every cell of your body is ready to conform. This is precisely the goal of an initiate, to win obedience of his own inner world. If we want to meditate we have to understand the nature of the psychic world. Meditation is a psychological and philosophical question. Spiritual work is not achieved through the intellect alone. Every single cell of your whole body should be involved as well as your emotional and mental body. You must learn to enjoy meditation. Meditation must become a need in you. In your minds, hearts and wills. You should look forward to those moments when you can immerse yourself in eternity and drink the Elixir of immortal life. See also the law of Meditation.

Margo Kirtikar Ph.D.

The Law of Present Moment

Time does not exist. What we know as past and future have no reality except in our own mental fabrication. The idea of time is a convention of thought and language, a human social agreement. The truth is we have only this one present moment. We keep the past alive when we hold a regret with our thoughts and feelings. The same is with the future. When we feel anxiety about the future and make it come alive through our imagination. Time is an abstract concept. In practicing remembrance that the here and now is all we have, our present moments improve and become moments of quality.

The Law of Privacy

This is a divine law that states that every person old and young, black, yellow or white, king or beggar is entitled to the sanctity of their own privacy. It is against this law to infringe on this right of individual privacy. Included in this infringement would be such things as mind reading without the person's consent or questioning their motives or thoughts concerning their personal lives without their consent.

Just think how often this law is violated individually and collectively and just how many individuals both young and old are robbed of their sense for privacy. Privacy is a part of becoming an independent person. When personal space, private thoughts and feelings are infringed upon personal freedom and progress is denied to the individual.

The Law of Process

This law is an awareness that we have things to accomplish in our life. If we wish to reach a certain goal, we must set a direction and create order, prepare well and proceed in small but sure steps. Any achievement can be managed in addition. Skipping a single step or taking a short cut often results in failure. Also included in this law is the knowing to appreciate the accomplishment of a step toward a goal.

The Law of Productivity

Turning the energy of our thoughts and of our work into a physical product is the process of productivity. Productivity brings growth and rewards.

Margo Kirtikar Ph.D.

The Law of Progress

Everything is either progressing or regressing. Nothing stands still. It is the basis of the phenomenon of sensation, which is the key to this solar system of love, our system being a 'Son of Necessity' or desire. This law is the working out into manifestation of the informing consciousness of a part of the Deva kingdom and of certain pranic energies. This law governs the vegetable kingdom and the Deva kingdom. It is the basis of the phenomenon of sensation, which is the key to this solar system of love our system being that of desire.

The Law of Projection

The law of Projection states that the film that projects, depicts, and creates the events of one's life story, is stored within one's consciousness, and can only be changed from within. The intimate conversations, attitudes, and the relationship one has within one's own consciousness, is reflected in experiences on the outer screen of life; one is both the camera and projector of his life story. Those who wish to see a world premier of new and joyous experiences instead of reruns, trash films, soap operas, tragedies, illness and hostilities, must refuse to bring or to allow such films, concepts or images to enter their theaters or be filed into their storage banks. Those who seek out, allow, or enjoy filming such trash do surely fill their cameras with the material that may eventually become part of their outward life.

Those who allow only the highest, clearest and the best thoughts, ideas, words, experiences and images to enter their studio shall create and project films that show a life of joy and art.

The Law of Prophecy

The only true future that exists is the desire or will of the Source of all Creation that none shall be lost and that the future is happening, unfolding in the 'I AM' now. Sacred geometry is an aspect, a manifestation of Gods's love. People who are able to tune into the Akashic records and into the Universal Consciousness are sometimes using sacred geometry to draw a line from the supposed past, present and to the future. The ability to use sacred geometry comes with the raising of vibration Akasha for the good of another or self. When reading the energy going to the future of people on earth one must keep in mind that this energy changes from moment to moment.

While those powerful prophets of old were correct in their time and some of what they said has held to present day much of their prophecies have lost relevancy. Just by hearing prediction, we change the outcome to some degree.

The Law of Prosperity

The law of Prosperity states that one prospers in direct proportion to the enjoyment one receives in seeing the prosperity of oneself and others. And that one's prosperity is denied in direct proportion to one's feeling of guilt for being prosperous, or at the envy and hostility one feels on witnessing other's prosperity.

This law states that when one prospers all may prosper. The law of Prosperity works for those who hold images, feelings, actions, dialogue, and attitudes associated with beauty, joy, love and prosperity. It works against those who hold images, feelings, actions, dialogues and attitudes associated with ugliness, self-pity, complaints, envy and hostility toward oneself or any other person, group, race, or class.

Those who think, feel, act and speak of themselves as being poor and needy must spend three times the energy for the same prosperity received by those who think, feel, act, and speak of themselves as being wealthy and prosperous. An attitude that dwells in depression leads to the way of physical, spiritual, mental, social and financial depression. Those who maintain prosperous attitudes, even in states of poverty, are foreign to such states and will not be allowed to remain out of place in those poverty situations, but will instead be deported to those prosperous states where such prosperous attitudes belong.

What we desire manifests only when we release any thoughts, words, deeds, intent, motive and actions to the contrary. Prosperity is our birthright and needs no justification.

Margo Kirtikar Ph.D.

Additionally we may keep in prosperity only that which we are willing to surrender and are assisting others to manifest also.

The Law of Purification

This is about purifying the self to gain contact to the higher spiritual world. A clean radiant aura is essential to draw those helpful godly elements near to you. Purifying your emotional body of all irritation, anger, fear and all other such negative lower emotional traits, developing soul qualities instead such as love, generosity, courage, integrity, patience, etc. Purifying the mental body of all the negative dark thoughts such as revenge, criticism, envy, hate, etc. which keep you chained down to the lower plane, and instead observing and being aware of the quality of your thoughts, your speech and your actions. Purifying the physical body by leading a healthy lifestyle, keeping a nourishing fresh diet of fruits, vegetables, grains and nuts rather than meat and dead food, purifying your environment by being aware of your surroundings and of the company you keep.

Music and in particular singing gives us the conditions most conducive to the purification and embellishment of our physical bodies. Every spiritual journey inevitably begins with a self purification process. See also the law of Sound.

Margo Kirtikar Ph.D.

The Law of Radiation

This law comes into activity in connection with the highest specimens of the various kingdoms and governs the radioactivity of minerals, the radiation of the vegetable kingdom and perfumes. Smell is the highest of the purely physical senses. It is the outer effect produced by all forms in all kingdoms when their internal activity has reached such a stage of vibratory activity that the confining walls of the form no longer form a prison, but permit the liberation of the subjective essence. Liberation means the ability of any conscious atom to pass out of one sphere of energized influence into another of a higher vibration of a larger and wider expanse of conscious realization.

The Law of Reality

The law of Reality is that law which is measured by empirical formulae, which are set up in relation to dimension. If an object can be seen, can be heard, can be measured, can be felt, then this object is said to have reality. This is a measurable idea, something in the dimension of time as well as the dimension of energy and the dimension of form.

Margo Kirtikar Ph.D.

The Law of Rebirth

The law of Rebirth is a natural law on our planet and is a process of progressive development enabling the human to move forward to spiritual perfection and intelligent perception to become a member of the Kingdom of God. This law is established and carried forward under the law of Evolution and is related to and conditioned by the law of Cause and Effect. It accounts for the differences among men and in connection with Karma it accounts for the differences in attitudes and circumstances of life. The law of Rebirth comes into activity upon the soul plane and incarnation is motivated and directed from the soul level, upon the mental plane.

It is under the law of Rebirth that man slowly develops the mind to control the emotions to reveal the soul, at which point the man begins to tread the Path or Return and orients himself gradually, after many lives, to the Kingdom of God. When the man has a state where he has a developed mentality, wisdom, practical service, understanding and has learned to ask nothing for the separated self and renounces desire for life in the three worlds he is freed from the law of Rebirth. At this point he is group conscious. See also the law of Consciousness. All souls incarnate and re-incarnate under the law of Rebirth.

This law, when understood correctly, will do much to solve the problems of sex and marriage and other relationships. It will create a person who treads more carefully on the path of life as each life is an assuming of ancient obligations. Each life is not only a summary of life experience, but also the unfolding of awareness, a recovery of old relations, an opportunity for the paying of old indebtedness, a chance to make restitution and progress, an awakening of deep-seated qualities and recognition of old friends and enemies. Each life is the solution of revolting injustices and the explanation of that which conditions man and woman and makes them what they are. The man can break the wheel of rebirth consciously to bring about his own liberation.

The Law of Rebound

The law of rebound concerns the right of one to come out of a negative situation stronger and bolder and with more soul growth than previously experienced. This has been used as an example in stories since the beginning of mankind. Traumatic situations create the need for rebound, and the soul then often seeks these negative occurrences to give self a leap in faith. This law works in this way too. If we take a ball and throw it against the wall and if we do not step aside it will bounce back and hit us.

The Law of Receiving

It is said, 'It is more blessed to give than to receive' and 'as you freely give, you freely receive.' This law cannot proceed to supply our needs without a pattern to work with. Many would say, 'Well, after I get, then I will give.' But the law works differently. If you want to receive good you must first give some good to build upon. You give and according to what you give you receive back. Some people say, 'Well I do give, and sometimes until it hurts, but I seldom see any sign of return.' There is a right way and a wrong way to give. There is careless impulsive giving, and there is careful, scientific giving. When we give impulsively we are retarding progress, we are wasting our substance. Where we give to one who doesn't put forth the effort to help himself, we need not expect a good return. Nature does not support a parasite or a loafer, but she gives her energy to the ones who are struggling forward. She lets the parasite and the loafer see that she will help if they put forth the effort to help themselves. But with us, if we support a loafer in what he is in, how can we expect any good returns? Rather the loafer becomes arrogant and demanding for more and more relief, until we wonder where and when it will end.

After we give, our next step is to prepare to receive the response or results of our giving and to receive, as the law states, 'good measure, pressed down, shaken together, and running over.' This is the exciting part, because our preparation shows our active faith. Instead of rocking and waiting, we are prepared and working. This in turn, enlarges our view. It stimulates our interest, it disperses our doubt and fear, and

Margo Kirtikar Ph.D.

energizes our power of reception. The key to this law is that we are continually drawing into life what we give and expect. Therefore our actions and intent whether well thought or careless will have an effect on what we receive.

The Law of Reconciliation

The law of Reconciliation allows those things which are normally in conflict to become harmonious in relationship to one another. The law of Reconciliation is that which finds in differing qualities unifying similarities that allows these differences to be brought together; to accept the unifying qualities and diminish the differences, so that the differences in the qualities become less clashing and conflicting and the unifying qualities become more binding. This is to reconcile, to find common denominators in things that are normally seen as separate, and to emphasize and exaggerate and promote those common denominators, thus allowing the differences to fade away, or fall into proper alignment. We can apply this law in our daily personal and professional relationships. To make your custom to look for the common denominator, to find common interests so that you can get along with someone, rather than to concentrate on the differences that exist. It is all a matter of changing your perspective. Open another window to look out from to get a different point of view of the world.

Margo Kirtikar Ph.D.

The Law of Reflection

'As above, so below.' Like a mirror the universe reflects back that which shines forth into it. On a practical level this also manifests in all our relationships. If we meet someone who reflects to us characteristics that we think we have or would like to have then we approve of this person. If the person reflects to us characteristics that we have that we dislike in ourselves or pretend not to have then we feel an immediate dislike to the person. So next time you feel this immediate like or dislike reflect on why you feel that way. On another level we can also think of this law as the world reflecting back to us like a mirror, the energies and the image and energies that we send out to the world.

The Law of Reincarnation

Reincarnation once agreed upon must play out to its natural conclusion unless one submits to the universal law of Planning to change its course. Reincarnation is not mandatory but the optional process once begun, will run its course. This law applies to the greatest majority of those of us in the physical world. In other words, the soul chooses the situation and the parents where it is born, according to the lessons that the soul has to learn. One of the reasons why a soul re-incarnates is to continue the perfection process upon the Earth, another is to satisfy some unfulfilled desire. But the most important reason is the will and knowledge of the Plan. The main incentive is sacrifice and service to those lesser lives that are dependent upon the higher inspiration of the spiritual soul. Contrary to general belief, it is usually group rebirth that is taking place all the time and incarnation of the individual is occasional in comparison. See also the law of Cyclic Returns, law of Rebirth, the law of Karma and the law of the Soul.

The Law of Relativity

This Awareness indicates that the law of Relativity is but the relationship of all things understood by the particular viewpoint from which they are seen. As the experience continues, greater awareness and the desire for more understanding increases. The entity, the force, man then begins to probe into the nature of those forces outside of its own control and understanding. This awareness indicates as this occurs, the quality of reason, the rational approach begins to develop. This awareness also indicates as the viewpoint shifts, the relative relationship of those things also becomes different. As an example a train moving at a particular rate of speed in relation to the entity standing beside the tracks, is somewhat different from the rate of speed of another train passing in the apposite direction, or of an automobile traveling in the same direction as the train. It all depends on where we stand in life and from which window we are looking through and how we feel at that particular moment. Each viewpoint is relative, and each is accurate, and yet the descriptions will be totally different.

The Law of Relaxation

In many cases the laws of mind are the reverse of the laws of matter. On the physical plane usually the more effort we make the more we achieve, for example the harder you hit a nail the quicker it will go into a piece of wood. It does not work like that on the mental plane. The moment you force something on the mental plane you create tension and when tense the mind cannot be creative. On the physical plane the quicker you walk or run the quicker you reach your destination. On the mental plane the more effort you make the less your result will have. You cannot force your mind to work faster because you will only create a mental block. You stop the creative energies flowing. You need to relax to let the energies flow freely so your mind can be creative. The idea is that you need to be relaxed but alert in all your mental work, unhurried and quiet, but focused, because effort defeats itself. All creative people are aware of this law and the way it operates.

The Law of Release

You are bound to that which you do not release. Release that which is holding you down. Let it go. Let go. Release it to the Higher Power to be released in minute, benign particles disseminating into the infinite universe. Release of useless desires opens the way for greater love. The release of love to others leads to a tenfold increase of love in our lives. We cannot keep it unless we give it away. All that is, belongs to all who are. Personal possession is a myth. One of the hardest things for us to do is to let go. Let go of old relationships or situations when they have served their purpose and stagnated. See also the law of Affinity and the law of Sympathy.

The Law of Repetition

Everything created repeats itself, every large cycle includes in its earlier stages, all the lesser, and repeats the earlier procedure. One good example is the human physical body, the fetus reproduces all earlier stages and forms until the human is achieved. Everything repeats itself.

Margo Kirtikar Ph.D.

The Law of Repulse

This is also known as the law of all destroying angels, and its symbol is an angel with a flaming sword, turning in all directions. It is the Angel guarding the treasure, driving man forth in search of another way of entrance, thus forcing him through the cycle of rebirth until he finds the portal of initiation.

The Law of Repulsion

In a similar manner, the law of repulsion can be stated this way. As you seek, you repel and are repelled by that which will not fulfill your search. You have created whatever exists in your life or is happening to you at this time. Through the laws of attraction and repulsion, coupled with your deep desires, you have brought that creation into your life to fulfill your present needs and desires.

Margo Kirtikar Ph.D.

The Law of Respect

The law of Respect is that principle of looking twice, or more precisely, looking twice as deeply for respect goes far beyond the surface appearance and superficial glances to discover a deeper meaning, purpose or basis for discovery.

Without the principle of respect, the 'Book of Love' will never be read, the 'Tree of Life' will never be seen in full bloom, and the thousands of rainbows of the 'Land of Essence' will never be viewed. But with the law of Respect in action, the mysteries of the universe, or any part, will open layer after layer, like the unfolding of a thousand petal lotus.

The Law of Respiration

Breath is the beginning and the end. Our life begins with our first breath and ends with our last breath and the mystery of life is to be found in respiration. Respiration is breathing in and out, contraction and expansion. Everything breathes, the Cosmos breathes, our earth breathes, oceans, stars, stones, trees and animals breathe, all breathe in their own way having their own rhythm. Respiration has a paramount importance in the life of every spiritualist. Ancient Indian Yogis and Sages have studied respiration in detail and state that the rhythm of breath when in harmony with the rhythm of earth can facilitate communication with certain parts of the spiritual world.

Regular breathing exercises will improve your health. Each individual has his own rhythm which he must find by listening to the inner doctor. Breathe slowly and rhythmically, focusing all your attention on the air coming into your lungs. Think of all the elements that it is bringing you for the benefit of your breath. When you draw air into your lungs, you must do so in the conscious conviction that you are receiving divine blessings with every breath you inhale. Breathing is also very important for the functioning of the brain and you should get into the habit of taking few deep breaths several times a day, to purify your blood which then supplies your brain with the elements it needs to function at its best. As you breathe out think that you are expanding to the very outer limits of the universe and as you breathe in again you withdraw inwards into the point at the center of an infinite circle. As you expand and contract you will discover the 'ebb and flow' which is the key to all the rhythms of the universe. When you become conscious of this movement within your own being, you enter into the harmony of the cosmos and thus establish a relationship, breathing in elements from space and breathing out a part of your heart and soul into space. The one who knows how to harmonize himself with the respiration of the cosmos enters into the sphere of divine consciousness. See also the law of Inverse Proportions.

The Law of Responsibility

The law of Responsibility states that one entity or more working in a manner that is responsive to the needs of many does receive energy from those many. The ability to respond to the needs of others allows that responsive entity energy from all those who await that response. This relates to The law of Co-Creation, yet it is somewhat different, for one being who is greatly responsive can have the power of 144 whose energies are simply utilized for their own personal interest.

It was the Creator's idea to separate, to give our Soul existence. It was our idea to go away from God into materiality with the original purpose of profound and speedy soul growth. There are some souls who have experienced, to some degree, soul loss. God is responsible for us through love and we are responsible to become or reclaim this Divine Love. Once we establish the limits and boundaries of our responsibility, we can take full charge of that which is our duty and let go of that which is not. We find more enjoyment supporting others as we create more harmonious cooperative relationships by understanding that which falls within our realm of responsibility.

Under this law we understand a person's need to over cooperate to such an extent that one becomes codependent—the condition which is obsessive focus on other peoples' lives. This law reminds us to respect our internal values and find our own point of balance. We are unfailingly responsible for every one of our thoughts, words, deeds, intents, motives and actions.

Margo Kirtikar Ph.D.

The Law of Revelation

God's Divine Plan is guaranteed to be revealed to those who have been prepared to and have agreed to receive it. In other words nothing is secret. All is there for us to know if we want to know.

The Law of Rhythm

Everything flows, out and in, in and out and through. Everything has its tides, all things rise and fall, the pendulum swing manifests in everything, the measure of the swing to the right is the measure or the swing to the left. Rhythm compensates. This principle, on the physical plane, is the most visible of all principles and its powers are observed within the forces of nature which move the waves and tides of our oceans and the continuous changes of the seasons. It is observed in the continuous cycles of life and death and the rebirth of all things. A constant creation and destruction of suns, worlds, and galaxies and in the rise and fall of governments and nations. On the plane of energy it is observed in the behavior of the alternating current wave of electricity, light and heat as it vibrates between the positive and negative pole. Rhythm on the mental plane is experienced as the wide mood swings displayed in human nature from extremes of happiness or sadness, gentle or violent.

Rhythm is the law of compensation and maintains the equilibrium in all things. It returns to us what we measure out in life. There is no escape from the immutable law. The law holds true whether we believe or not and compensates us accordingly. All of nature follows this law. Rhythm perpetuates the phenomenon of time. There is a time for everything. The pendulum like swing of the rhythm is immutable and we can only counteract its backward swing by mentally polarizing ourselves in a desirable position on the scale of life. It requires a dedicated personal commitment to cultivate the unknown within all of us, in order to cause a quantum leap in the evolutionary process of life with all its aches and pains. This is a mental art that is known to hierophats, adepts and masters of all ages.

We will fulfill this law one way or another. We either use the law to our advantage or we become its subject. The door of universal law swings in all directions. The final result depends on what we have chosen to believe and whether or not our belief system allows us to see the truth as it really is. If we do not want to know or we do not care then we will evolve through the standard process of evolution. Nothing can, or is allowed to stand still in life. All manifestation is the result of active energy producing certain results, and expenditure of energy in any one direction will necessitate an equal expenditure in an apposite direction. Everything flows in rhythm. Rhythm is a spiritual reality.

The Law of Right Human Relations

This law helps us define limits of our behavior control with others. Everything is within us. Let no one assume to forcibly teach, counsel or guide by force. While each teacher is in a manner a director, the individual person may only be a means not a way of life. A strong action may promote refusal and achieve rejection, or it may encourage one to become dependent on another's will. By not searching for excellence within, one refuses the gifts already there but not recognized or realized. We achieve greater results in our relationships with others by our own fine example and also by listening. People answer their own questions if given enough opportunity. The only real control we ever have and need to have is with self.

Margo Kirtikar Ph.D.

The Law of Right to one's Space

This is an aspect of free will but another law of its own. Everyone is entitled to make decisions for self, decide the belief system one feels comfortable with and generally create the life that will allow one to fulfill his or her own birth vision. This is the right to one's own space, the right to live one's own life, allowing for parental direction to the developing young person. Over protective or controlling parents, friends and even dictators have impeded this law and right since almost the inception of mankind. In accordance with this law no one has the right to influence or infringe on someone else's space and life.

The Law of Ritual and Ceremony

The law of Ritual has to do with the importance of ceremonial ritual as a protective safeguard to the etheric body. The health of the physical body is dependent on the health of etheric body. Signs of ill health begin with the etheric body and when this is neglected manifests eventually in the physical body. Medical science does not recognize this fact as yet. Through ceremonial ritual with colors, smells and sound vibrations we can heal and/or maintain the etheric body.

Rituals and ceremonies are an important part of our life as we celebrate all meaningful occurrences and special dates in history, births, marriages, deaths and other. The use of candles, incense, offerings, gifts, prayers, songs, dances, all have their meaning, place and time. We have lost much in our modern times, unfortunately, as we tend to belittle all old rituals and ceremonies as having no meaning and beliefs are taken as 'superstition.' To mark certain special occasions in one's life through ritual and ceremony shared with loved ones and friends who add to the positive joyful energies activates the elements and entities in the universe to work with us on the psychic level and to bless the event. Throughout the ages rituals and ceremonies have been important to mankind and this continues to be so today.

The Law of Sacrifice

The law of Sacrifice is one of the seven laws of the Solar System. This law determines the nature of each kingdom. Each kingdom is meant to be a laboratory wherein are prepared the various forms of nutrition which are needed for the building of the more evolved and refined structures. So the plant world feeds from the minerals. Animals feed off the minerals and plants and the humans who are still more refined feed on all three. For the early stage of human development it was correct and necessary for the human to feed off the animal world. But this is not the case any more. The more refined the human development is the less need there is to feed off the animal world.

The principle of sacrifice is to be found on every level in the process of evolution. That which is lower is always sacrificed, in order to transform to that which is higher and more refined. In the human family for example, through death the principle of life is renounced and sacrificed and returns to the reservoir of universal life.

The law of Sacrifice and the law of Compensation are closely associated, but the first to be active and to be recognized in daily living is sacrifice. Compensation comes later. Put more simply something has always to be sacrificed in order to get something else. One can say there is a price for everything. Or, the compensation we receive is in accordance to the sacrifice we are willing to make. On a practical level for us it works in the same way on all levels. Our sacrifices would be a commitment or an investment of our time, energy and hard work for example in order to achieve a certain goal. Nothing is gained for free. In every day language we say: No pain no gain. The pain would be the sacrifice.

It is important to understand that 'sacrifice' here has no relation to the word sacrifice as we have so far understood it to be, as in blood sacrifices and offerings of killings of humans or animals. The sacrifice meant here has absolutely nothing to do with bloodshed. Divinity does not demand blood sacrifice.

Margo Kirtikar Ph.D.

The Law of Sacrifice and Death

Death is the controlling factor on the physical plane. The destruction of the form, in order that evolving life may progress, is one of the fundamental methods of evolution. This law is linked to the law of Disintegration. This controls the gradual disintegration of the form and its sacrifice to evolving life. See also The law of Sacrifice.

The Law of Schools

This law also known as the law of Love and Light is primarily applicable to all units of divine life who have arrived at, or transcended the stage of self-consciousness. It consequently deals with the Human Kingdom and there is a significance in this being law eleven. It is the law that enables one to unite two of one's aspects, the personal self with the Higher Self. It is the law which governs the transition of the human atom the physical into another and a higher kingdom. It is the law of the perfected human that when comprehended enables man to enter into a new cycle. Mankind is now at a stage where a number of units are ready to come under the specific influence of this law and thus to be transferred out of the Hall of Learning, via the Hall of Wisdom into the fifth Spiritual Kingdom.

This law concerns the great experiment which has been inaugurated on earth by our Planetary Logos in connection with the process of Initiation and does not concern all members of the human family, some of whom will achieve initiation slowly, under the basic law of Evolution. As there are various planetary schemes, each scheme exists in order to teach a specific aspect of consciousness and each planetary school or Hierarchy subjects its pupils to this law in diverse manners. There exists five great planetary school groups.

Margo Kirtikar Ph.D.

The Law of Security

The law of Security is that law which provides a foundation upon which an entity stands; whereby the entity can choose a form of expression that allows his or her best performance without infringing on the security or expression of others who have the same rights.

The Law of Service

The law of Service grows naturally out of the successful application of the sciences of the antakharana and meditation, and is the governing law of the future. With the linking of soul and personality the Light of the Soul pours into the brain consciousness, resulting in the subordination of the lower self to the higher self. This identification produces a corresponding activity in the personal life and the activity we call service. There in lies the growth through the service of the human race, and through a cultivated self-forgetfulness. Service is the true science of creation and is a scientific method of establishing continuity.

This is also known as the law of water and of fishes. The symbol is a pitcher on the head of a man who stands in the form of a cross. This law is the governing factor of the age of Aquarius. The ray energy is out going energy of the sixth ray, vivifying factor. If the evasion of this law is a conscious action, there are karmic penalties. This work requires so much sacrifice of time and personal interest, requiring deliberate effort conscious wisdom and the ability to work without attachment.

First there is service of the personality wherein one sacrifices much in the interest of one's own desires. Next comes the stage of service to humanity and finally the service to the plan. See also the law of Sacrifice.

The Law of Sex

This is the term applied to the force which brings about the physical merging of the two poles in connection with the human kingdom and of the animal kingdom, viewing him as responsive to the call of his and her animal nature. It concerns itself with the due guarding of the form in this particular cycle and its perpetuation. This sex force attraction is only powerful during the period of the duality of the sexes and their separation and in the case of the human will be offset by a higher expression of the law when man is again androgynous.

On the physical level, in the same manner that we eat and absorb physical food, astral food is absorbed by our psychic body. This means that when two people are in a deep embrace, a process of absorption takes place in the electromagnetic dimension of their beings, in their emanations, a process in which each one absorbs the weaknesses as well as the strengths of the other.

The Law of Silence

The law or Principle of Silence is that which allows beings the space, peace and time to rest and recuperate from the noises and chatter. The silence is found within the soul, and is not limited to sound, but also relates to silence in terms of motion, emotion and feeling. The law of Silence contains also the chaos that can exist in any moment when that chaos is experienced from levels of non-resistance. There are those who chatter endlessly and sometimes without meaning. Some find it very hard when they have to be silent and so resist. It is when one can be silent and can live within, be at peace with the self that one can listen to the higher divine impressions. One also needs to put a stop to the endless meaningless chatter going on in one's head. To be more in control of one's thoughts and be aware of the quality of the constant inner silent dialogue that goes on in one's head. It is when you are in control that you can experience an inner silence, enabling you to hear the Voice of Silence, the Voice of God and the Music of the Higher Spheres.

Margo Kirtikar Ph.D.

The Law of Simplicity

While the perception of complication exists in the lower mind, with God all things are simple. Therefore confusion does not exist. God is most easily understandable and such understanding is available to all. It is through development and refinement of one's higher faculties that one can understand this simplicity.

The Law of Solar Evolution

This law is the sum total of all lesser activities.

Margo Kirtikar Ph.D.

The Law of Solar Union

This is an occult term used when the interplay of the suns is being dealt with from the material aspect and from the consciousness aspect.

The Law of Soul

Matter is the vehicle for the manifestation of soul on the physical plane of existence, and soul is the vehicle on a higher plane for the manifestation of spirit. Through the use of matter the soul unfolds and find its climax in the soul of man. The individual soul is created out of Spirit with an ability to have free will, to make its own choices, to have its own opinions, intelligence, imagination and creativity. Soul is eternal with no beginning and no end and this means that when a person ceases to exist on this physical level, the soul continues to exist on a higher plane. The soul is the intermediate between the personality and the Spirit. Soul consciousness lives in all that exists on earth in different grades for example, it exists at its lowest form in minerals, and at its highest in the developed human being. We are eternally related to the souls of all men and we have a definite relationship to those who reincarnate with us, who are learning with us the same lessons, who are experiencing life and experimenting with us. It is the soul in all forms which reincarnates, choosing and building suitable physical, emotional and mental vehicles through which to learn the next needed lessons. Souls incarnate in groups cyclically under the law and in order to achieve right relations with God and their fellowmen. Progressive unfoldment, under the law of Rebirth, is largely conditioned by the mental principle, for 'as a man thinketh in his heart, so is he.'

The soul is neither spirit nor matter but is the relation between them. The soul is the mediator and the link between God and His form. The soul is the form building aspect that drives all God's creatures forward along the path of evolution. The qualities, vibrations, colors and characteristics in all the kingdoms of nature are soul qualities and these are brought into being through the interplay of the pairs of opposites, spirit and matter and their effect upon each other. The individual self, conscious soul is an integral part of the universal soul and when one has become aware of this fact one can intelligently cooperate with the will of God and work with the plan of evolution.

Humanity is an expression of two aspects of the soul the animal and the divine, these two fused in the human being make the human soul. It is through a long struggle and the sublimation of the animal soul that the divine soul is liberated. The two qualities of the soul are serenity and joy as the man and woman know that he and she is life itself. The more we think of each other as souls and not as limited human beings and as our love for humanity increases and love of the self decreases we will move towards the center of light and love and God. See also the law of Reincarnation, the law of Cyclic Returns, the law of Vibration, and the Soul's Journey.

The Law of Sound

Every living thing in existence has a sound. Through this knowledge changes will be brought about and new forms developed through its medium. The release of energy in the atom is linked to the science of sound. Healing with sound is profoundly effective be it vocal sounds, tuning forks or music. Sound has the power to restore people to their harmonic patterns. Chanting specific sounds and mantrams brings about great healing and raising of vibration and produces virtually unimaginable results when done with group mantric chanting. The most powerful mantra known to present man is OM MANI PADME HUM.

Each sound each vibration triggers a movement in space and releases certain forces in man. The sounds we hear produce geometrical figures within us which are real enough even if we cannot see them. The effect of sound, the vibratory energy of the waves it creates, causes myriads of minute particles in us that arrange themselves into geometrical figures. This is why when we listen to inharmonious music or very loud sounds the preexistent structure and harmony within us, the order that was established by the Creator, is disturbed and eventually shattered causing disharmony, disease and chaos in our life.

It is said in the words of an occult manual on healing: 'He who lives under the sound of the AUM knows himself. He who lives sounding the OM knows his brother. He who knows the SOUND knows all.'

Music, in particular singing, is a form of nourishment for the soul, which enables us to work on a spiritual level if it is done with awareness. The Logos is pure music, the harmonious sounds that fashioned the universe and sound models matter and gives it form. Under the influence of the Logos the Cherubim who reign on this level, received a divine vibration, which was communicated to all creatures below, all the way down to earth. The Cherubim do nothing but sing together in harmony and when humans also try to sing in harmony they create a bond between themselves and the Cherubims, the angelic order of music and heavenly harmony. When you sing, therefore, whether you know it or not, you are establishing contact with the Cherubims and the harmony of sounds causes the material particles of your body to vibrate in harmony and to heal. Singing is an expression of our desire to embrace the universe, to be attuned to and in harmony with the whole.

From a spiritual Master we learn that four part choral singing is of great significance for the blending of voices is at the same time a blending of our souls and spirits. It is a reflection of the effort we have to make every day, to bring our spirit, soul, mind and heart into a harmonious unity. The four voices, bass, tenor, contralto and soprano, correspond to the four strings of a violin, for a violin is also a symbol of man. The G-string represents the heart, the D-the intellect, the A-the soul, and the E-represents the spirit. The violin itself represents the physical body and the bow represents the 'will' that plays on the four principles—heart, mind, soul and spirit. The harmonious blending of the four voices or tones played, is a reminder that all the four principles in the human must vibrate in harmony within.

With the rhythmic in and out flow of breathing sound is produced. On the basis of this the process of breathing has been given the name of sound. Scriptures like the Vedas and Puranas are present in the sound and the art of singing is also based on the sound. The pattern of our breathing has a profound importance in our life. No wealth is worth more than sound and no knowledge is superior than the knowledge of the sound. Sound is like a great lamp that lights the soul.

Margo Kirtikar Ph.D.

The Law of Speech

We are the only species privileged with the Word. There is power in the spoken word. Thought forms the blueprint for reality, and speaking power into the blueprint brings that thought into the physical world. To say something is to make it real. One ought to watch every word that one speaks. Words are sound and vibrations that are energy sent out in to the world. When you speak you decree to manifest that in to the material world. When we speak in anger, contempt or abuse, we cause more damage than we think because we are sending out these negative energies into the atmosphere that go far beyond our immediate environment. In a way one can pollute the environment with words spoken in anger and with foul abusive language. We all ought to think before we speak.

One spiritual Master said: "The law of Spiritual Chemistry is the law transmuting all conditions, all vibrations, all darkness into beauty, music and light. One must learn to speak the language of the Angels. One must learn to speak from the soul. The one who speaks with the lips chatters, she/he speaks from an empty mind and adds confusion to discord. The one who speaks with the full mind feeds the minds of men. The one who speaks from the heart wins the confidence of mankind. But the one who speaks from the soul heals the heartbreaks of the world and feeds the hungry, the starving souls of mankind. She/he can dry the tears of anguish and pain. The one who speaks from the soul brings light for she/he carries light. The language of the soul is sacred and most beautiful. It is the language of the eternal spheres and the language of the Gods.

It is the gift of the spirit known as the 'new tongues.' The power of transmutation is the power to contact the center of the soul through the heart. This method alone holds the power of fulfillment and perfection." See also the law of Change.

Margo Kirtikar Ph.D.

The Law of Spiral Movement

Movement, change, growth succeeds in a spiral motion, souls circle the truth as souls ascend.

The Law of Spirit

Spirit is the principle of increase. There is always something more to come, another experience to experience and future conditions grow out of present conditions. Every human being has this deep instinct within him to seek something better. Spirit is the all penetrating power which is the forming power of the universes and the spirit works through souls. Self mastery simply means that a person has the ability to run his own life according to the laws of Spirit presuming of course that the person understands the laws. The understanding of these laws comes through the Light and Sound of God as a direct infusion into the soul. The spirit has many sounds, a sound like a rushing wind, or the sound of the flute amongst many others. 'Sound' and 'Light' are the twin aspects of spirit, the 'Voice of God.' When we experience the 'Voice of God' it means we have contact with the divinity. God is 'Being' and the 'Spirit' is an extension of this 'Being' into all universes and you are the instrument spirit made flesh.

No immortal art can ever be produced by a human being without inspiration from the Spirit. No one can produce divine works of art that inspire humanity, if one is not inhabited by heavenly beings.

The Law of Spiritual Approach

This law depicts the conscious act of a personality to create with its every thought, word and deed the ability to be the reflection of its God self. Every action is a prayer to the Creator of All. When this is done with success, the personality becomes a mirror or reflection of the God self for others to learn from and emulate. This is a walking, talking example of becoming our Higher Self.

The Law of Spiritual Awakening

A basic level of self-control and stability is required to maintain the degree of effort required for the awakening of other states of awareness. Because such awakening brings with it higher forms of perception and power, self-centered misuse of the greater perception and power bears proportionally graver karmic consequences. Spiritual awakening brings with it the need for moral impeccability.

Margo Kirtikar Ph.D.

The Law of Spiritual Non Perfection

According to the law of Non Perfection no one ever becomes a perfect being. There is no such thing as a perfect being because there is always one more step in the plan of conscious evolution. This is all the more true of spiritual things that always seek and never find completion.

The Law of the Subconscious Mind

The law of the Sub-Conscious Mind is not able to distinguish fact from fiction. If it is convinced a false statement is true, it will act as if it were true. If it is convinced a hot ember is cool, it will not experience a burn. If convinced a piece of ice is red hot, it will experience a burn. If convinced you are a failure, it will make sure that you fail. If it receives conflicting data, it will produce conflicting results. If it is convinced that you can do great and near impossible feats, it will act to make these things occur. It is truly the 'Genie in the bottle' which grants your wishes according to the 'commands' you give it in the intimate conversations you have with yourself. Understanding this law gives you the power to take the course of your life into your own hands by changing the perceptions and beliefs of your subconscious mind. Now you know why it is quite possible to walk on hot embers and not get burnt.

The subconscious mind uses all the knowledge that you have ever collected and probably have forgotten about to make things come true for you once it has accepted an idea. It mobilizes all your mental powers whether you are conscious of them or not. If used negatively it brings trouble, failure and sickness and if used positively it brings success, healing and freedom.

The Law of Substitution

This is an important mental law and has to do with thought control. It means that we can have only one thought at a time and the only way for us to get rid of the one thought is to substitute it by another. We cannot hold two thoughts in our head at the same time. It is either one or the other. So if we want to get rid of a negative thought the only way for us to do that is to think of something positive. If we want to stop thinking about one thing in particular then we must turn our attention to something else in order to replace the first thought that has occupied our mind.

Sometimes it helps to engage oneself with activities such as sport, a movie, a book or music to take one's mind off the problem or negative thought. Do not say or think 'I don't want to think about this' because that would make it only worse. It works better if you just turn your attention to something else. After you have taken a little distance you will find it easier to deal with the problem effectively.

The Law of Suggestion

The law of Suggestion states that a statement carries with it an impact associated with the law of Description. When given through certain levels of consciousness and moments of expression and situations of experience, such suggestions may have a terrific impact upon the psyche of oneself or another. See also the law of Penetration.

The Law of Summons

Otherwise known as soul talk, one can learn how to lift the soul from the physical body and summon another soul, to have a soul to soul talk. This is most powerful because there is no conscious ego present. The message of love and or explanation or plea is received in a most profound manner.

The Law of Supply

Man is never satisfied. This fact is deplored by many but God did not intend that man should be forever satisfied. The law of his being is perpetual increase, progress and growth; so, when one good is realized, another desire for a greater good will develop and when a higher state is reached, another and more glorious state will unfold his vision and urge him on and on. Hence, the advancing life is the true life, the life that God intended man to live. The law of good is universal, for, are we not all seeking good in some form or another? Science and logic alike declare that the universe is filled with the essential substance of every imaginable good that man can image, and that he is entitled to a full and ever increasing supply of any and every good he may need or desire. We believe, therefore, that it is right and good for man to seek to gratify all pure desires and ambitions. 'What things so ever ye desire, when ye pray, believe that ye receive them and ye shall have them.'

Every person, consciously or unconsciously, is operating this law in one or more of its phases. It works universally and on every plane of life's expression. We are all daily drawing into our lives the things we most desire and expect, and whether we attract good things or bad things, the principle operated is the same. But as we want more of the good things in life and less of the bad, it will be necessary to understand the law more perfectly, and so be able to adapt our thinking to it in a more direct fashion. Thus we secure the greater benefits that accrue from a conscious, intelligent use of its power. The secret of this law lies in our consciousness. Our life consists not in the abundance of the things we possesses, but in the consciousness of that which we have.

If we meet with limitations in our life we need not be anxious or worry about it because worry and fear tend to restrict and limit the supply at hand. They tend to close off the outflow of substance, whether that flow is small or large. Instead of lifting us out of limitation and instead of improving our conditions or increasing our supply they drag us deeper into the throes of doubt and fear. Instead of expecting more to follow, we grow tense and anxious, which increases our fear and brings us less and less. Instead of tightening up our thinking, we must relax and be more expanding. We must educate our minds to a larger state of thinking.

When we can think and realize more abundance, we shall receive more abundantly. According to the law of Supply the more man grows in true knowledge and the more he uses his power in constructive ways, the more good he will create in the circle of his expression and in his own little world.

The Law of Surrender

Because people so cherish the self, surrendering is a very frightening experience. A person may experience surrender as a leap into an abyss or as death. This may be perceived by one who has not yet attained a complete trust and faith in God, the complete assurance that once the self is abandoned, the being automatically merges with a higher stage of existence which is ready and waiting to accept it. There is no chance for the process not to function. At the instant of surrender, the entire being of the individual merges into the specific higher manifestation of reality that its in relation to at that point in its development. God streams into the soul that has managed to negate the self. This is the surrender of the idea of the 'I', the ego.

Often this process of surrendering to ego is misunderstood as killing the ego. In fact a developed ego or personality is essential, for the spiritual path. The surrender is nothing but the recognition by the ego of the higher self and accepting the soul to be the inner Master.

Margo Kirtikar Ph.D.

The Law of Symbols

Symbols carry the meaning of messages from our guides. Esoteric knowledge was always throughout the ages and worldwide given out in symbols and codes so only the worthy could understand them. Every symbol has a meaning.

Here are some examples. The dot is the basic symbol of the infinitesimal and supreme power. All the subsequent geometrical forms or shapes are believed to be developed from the dot. A line is presumed to be a symbol of the power that began creation. The vertical stroke represents the oneness of God, the power descending from above, or the yearning of mankind for higher things. The horizontal stroke represents the earth in which life flows evenly and everything moves on the same plane. The sign of the cross means God and earth are combined in harmony. In occultism the perfect power or the motion of the life element has been explained by triangle. Three dots the form, and the motion, or power, make up the triangle. A triangle also depicts the entire trio that pertain to creation, three Virtues (Triguna), Trinity (Trideva), three elements (Tritatva), three words (Triloka), three Gods (Devatrayes). The triangle represents a Pythagorean symbol for wisdom the triple personality in man and it also represents the female element which is firmly based upon terrestrial matters and yet yearning for higher things. The triangle standing upon its apex is, on the other hand, represents the male element which is by nature celestial and strives after truth.

When we place the two triangles on top of each other to form a six pointed star, it represents the perfect human being who has achieved divinity. The five pointed star is Solomon's seal representing the five senses and for the Jews it represents also the five Mosaic Books. In ancient times it was a magic charm amongst the people of Babylon. The square is the emblem of the world and the four elements in nature. The cube unfolded is in display a cross of TAU, or Egyptian form, or the Christian cross form. The symbol 'Y' or fork, is a Pythagorean emblem of the course of life, in the form of a rising path with fork roads leading to Good and Evil. It is also a sign of the expectant soul gazing aloft with outstretched arms. The same 'Y' sign upside down expresses salvation descending from above and spreading over the world below. The combined dot form of Shiva and Shakti expands to assume the shape of a circle or ring for the sake of creation. The circle without a beginning or an end also represents God or Eternity. A circle with a dot in the middle is the open eye of God and God said 'Let there be Light.'

Margo Kirtikar Ph.D.

The Law of Synthesis

This is one of the three major Cosmic Laws. Also known as the law of Life. The law of Synthesis is the basic law of the positive pole. We would need to develop Buddhic faculty in order to comprehend this law. This law demonstrates the fact that all things abstract and concrete exist as one; it is the law governing the thought form of that One of the cosmic Logoi in Whose consciousness both our system and our greater center, have a part. It is a unit of His thought, a thought form in its entirety, a 'concrete whole' and not the differentiated process that we feel our evolving system to be. It is the sum total, the center and the periphery, and the circle of manifestation regarded as a unit. The motivating urge of God, His outstanding desire is towards union and at-one-ment of soul and matter, soul and spirit. The trend to synthesis is an instinct inherent in the entire universe, to which man is only awakening.

The trend of all evolutionary processes today is guided by the idea of synthesis: Global planning, international relationships, economic fusion, interdependence, the welfare of humanity as a whole, sharing of commodities all of which alleviate separation, isolation and division. See also the law of Life.

The Law of Teaching

This law concerns the responsibility people have to pass on the knowledge which they learn, for the continuation of the human race who can benefit by this information, when it is in the higher interest of people to learn the acquired information. However, learning to some extent is passed on through the genes, however, this is a physical materialization of inner knowledge achieved and retained from past lives. The human being does not erupt with a clean slate into existence at birth and then laboriously begin its first attempt to gain experience. If this were the case, we would still be back in the Stone Age.

Incarnated advanced souls on the physical plane receive training and instructions at night directly from the Masters or from some of the great devas at night. These classes are usually imparted in small groups or individually on the mental plane. To be able to receive and to interpret the physical impressions a perfect steadiness of inner poise on the part of the advanced soul is imperative. The aspirant must retain peace at all times, inner serenity, free from all daily turmoil and keep the mind agile. This is a hard and rigorous training and requires the student to practice self discipline, be free of all criticism, unnecessary questioning or emotional instability. The focus is on the control of the physical instrument i.e. the physical body.

The science of meditation and the building of the antahkarana, the bridge of light between the personality and the soul, are the two preliminary stages on the esoteric curriculum. The relation of the individual soul to all souls is taught and the recognition that the long awaited kingdom of

God is simply the appearance of soul controlled men and women on earth, in everyday life and at all stages of control on the physical level. When this relationship is recognized and more advanced souls and initiates come into power, the fact of the spiritual hierarchy will be accepted. The realization will be there that the kingdom of God has always been present on earth, but has remained unrecognized, owing to the few people who actually express the divine qualities of the soul. When this knowledge has spread and is present in the human consciousness everywhere, the presence of the divine soul qualities will then be regarded as normal, and the divine plan of evolution will be recognized.

The teachings and spiritual impressions of spiritual Masters, Krishna, Buddha, Christ and other spiritual world teachers in the past have not been expressed as was hoped for, as mankind in general lacked the self knowledge and the needed self discipline, and the majority were ruled by personal greedy desires and selfish ambitious motives. See also the law of Education, the law of Soul, the law of Reincarnation, the law of Rebirth and the law of Evolution.

The Law of Telepathy

The will, projected from the point between the eyebrows, the third eye, the Ajna center, is known as the broadcasting apparatus of thought. When the feeling is calmly concentrated on the heart it acts as a mental radio and can receive the messages of others from far or near. In telepathy the fine vibrations of thoughts in one person's mind are transmitted through the subtle vibrations of astral ether and then through the earthly ether, creating electrical waves which then translate themselves into thought waves in the mind of another person. This is normally done instantaneously.

Telepathy actually is in constant operation. Whatever our thoughts are about others and about ourselves they materialize as such in our world. If we expect someone to behave badly then for sure they will. If we see the best in someone then the person will give his best. Our thoughts and feelings are picked up even when unspoken, by the sub conscious of whomever they are directed to and will influence their behavior. True telepathy is a direct mental communication from mind to mind and in its more advanced expression is a communication from soul to soul. See also the law of Thought, the law of Meditation and the law of Akasha.

The Law of Tenfold Return

The law of Tenfold Return is that universal principle wherein gifts freely given for spiritual use return to the grantor good fortune equal to or greater than ten times the loss. This law works on the principle that when a vacuum is created it must be filled, when a seed is magically planted, it will bear fruit greater than its weight and original value. This law states that when you give freely, you can expect to receive ten times what you have given, thus enabling you to give ten times more. Practicing the law of Tenfold Return will help you to create an attitude and experience of wealth.

The Law of Thought

This awareness indicates there is an old occult law which humans may benefit from understanding. This law states 'energy follows thought.' Through focused mental thought one can manifest things on the physical plane. Every thought no matter how trivial sends out energy into the universe, colored with the quality of that specific thought, and which will eventually manifest in the material world. If we have constructive thoughts, then good will manifest on the physical plane, if however, we have destructive thoughts then only evil can manifest. Those who wish to energize need only to direct their thoughts toward that target which needs energizing. This requires of course the ability to focus and great concentration power. There is power in the thought and when thoughts remain unharnassed havoc is created in our environment. This shows us how important it is that we are aware of what we think and that our thoughts need to be guided by the soul within. We can gain control of our thought faculty through developing our mind. Through the practice of meditation we can develop the faculties of the mind and establish the union of body mind and soul, to acquire soul qualities so that our thoughts are guided by the soul.

Contrary to general esoteric belief thought power alone cannot heal. Thought can be the directing agency of forces and energies, which can disrupt or eliminate disease, but the process must be aided by the power to visualise, by the ability to work with forces and the ability to handle light substance.

Margo Kirtikar Ph.D.

Thought alone neither cures disease nor causes it. See also the law of Meditation, the law of Telepathy and the law of Healing.

The Law of Three

Every event requires three forces in order to occur. There is a positive or active force, a negative or passive force, and a neutral or reconciling force, also known as first, second and third force respectively. We must see this in the simplest circumstances of life.

As an example, imagine yourself lying in bed early morning. Your intellect is saying, "It's time to get up!". Your instinct is saying, "Just five more minutes." This tug-of-war may go on for some time with nothing happening. You lie motionless in bed, experiencing the push and pull between the active, first force and the denying, second force. Suddenly you see the time and realize you will be late for work. The emotional center interjects, "Oh my God, I'm going to be late." You jump out of bed, propelled into action. A third or reconciling force has entered. The first force can be seen as desire, the second force as resistance to that desire. These are readily apparent to us in the play of life. We do not, however, so readily perceive the existence of the third force. It is said we are blind to the third force. It is an aspect of our sleep, as Gurdjeff would say, our existence in the realm of duality, that we are unaware of Third Force.

In the second state of consciousness, waking sleep, we are incapable of thinking beyond duality. We engage almost completely in form thinking. Remember, this term denotes our tendency to think in two's, yes and no, left or right, this way or that. It also is referring to our inability to see beyond form to grasp the substance the form contains. So we become stuck in what seems to be contradictions. We are constantly engaged in the struggle between yes and no and fail to perceive the third alternative that has the power to solve the dilemma.

The Law of Three Requests

Whenever we pray or request a Higher Power to assist us, we bring stronger energy to the effort by repeating our request prayer three times over.

The Law of Time

The only moment we have is now. This is where we create, what we have done is done and that moment in history exists only as a record or energy trace in time and space. The consequences of past actions are atoned through karma and can be rewritten to a degree. The future only ever happens in and from the present tense and is built on today's thoughts dressed by emotion and driven by action. Activity is the key.

Third dimension living has more rigid structure of time than fourth dimension existence. There are those who can slip into 'no time' but these are people who have raised their personal vibration by demonstrating many virtues and have dispensed a great deal of karma and much killing of their ego and accessed the information to create the ability. Third dimension linear time was created for those living under this veil of forgetfulness to center in the moment and perceive a sense of order without the remembrance of burdens of past lives.

The Law of Tolerance

The law of Tolerance allows us to recognize the divinity in others even when covered by their masks and armor of demonic imagery and activities, or hidden behind the walls of apparent ignorance, sleep, and stupidity; or residing in the bowels of lust, greed, and power. The law of Tolerance is that law which allows one to speak through these walls and barriers to the divine God-Cell which lies buried behind these outer layers, and awaits liberation from the deep confines and imprisonment at the center of the self. This awareness suggests you are all gods, and must in time learn to speak to each other as though you were addressing Gods.

The Law of Truth

Truth being a vibration of the highest frequency, always prevails, it can be subverted temporarily, but will always prevail. Truth being absolute however does have levels of frequency. See the law of Paradox and the law of Spiral Movement.

The Law of Unconditional Love

This is a condition as well as a law of third dimension living. Loving ourselves and other people as they are, is honoring self and another's self and soul path. It is loving without judgment or reservation, without any selfish motive with the awareness that we are all part of God or the All. When we love without condition or restraint we connect in a profound manner with our own Higher Self. We notice that we say the right things at the right time in our communication with others while loving unconditionally. Life and events seem to flow to us in a more joyous and agreeable manner. Everything seems easy when living in unconditional love.

The Law of Unfulfillment

The law of Eternal Unfulfillment states that there never can be completion or fulfillment in any moment. For if there were, there would be no further movement; and as each moment contains within itself all that is essential for that moment, so also each moment contains within itself an emptiness, an unfulfillment that is essential and necessary to lead into the next moment.

The law of Eternal Unfulfillment states that every moment has something missing and is incomplete, and every moment has something that is present, total and complete; and when one accepts this law, the greed-creating obsession to be fulfilled will cease to be.

The Law of Unity

The law of Unity is a law which recognizes no separateness, which ignores the appearance and the illusion of separateness in the apparent divisions of polarities, gender, the one and the many; realizing these each as integrated parts of the total picture. This law is about thinking of the whole instead of the parts. The western mind is usually accustomed to think in terms of the parts rather than the whole. Most people think in fragments and are, therefore, unable to detach to step back in order to look at the picture as a whole.

The law of Unity identifies with the over-all viewpoint and does not see for example night and day as separate but as a night-day process. It does not recognize right or wrong as two separate entities but as one process of right and wrong. It does not see pleasure and then pain, but the pleasure-pain process. It does not see the one nor the all, but the At-One-Ment process of the ALL One Being, whose cells and souls work together even in the seemingness of division.

The law of Unity acknowledges such division, but stresses the oneness of the parts. The law of Unity sees loss and gain, life and death as nothing but the spinning wheel of fortune that is based on the law of Change, which is itself a unified process known as the law of Magic. To apply this law in our daily life, we can each day experience the different natures of our fellow humans and the other forms of life we relate with. We accept these differences as part of the Creator's universal design. We use our inner feelings to experience the unity that connects all things regardless of their outward appearance and behavior.

The Law of Unity and Separation

The law of Unity and Separation is the foundation of all wisdom and knowledge. It reveals the big picture of how the universe is structured and how it operates. Elements unite and elements separate. Once individual particles (matter) came into existence, two basic processes began. Growth, the uniting of individual particles and decay, their separation. These ongoing actions ensure that continuous change is the natural state of the Universe. Eventually life in its present form will cease and the divisions in the Universe will no longer exist. At that point the Universe will return to its original state of unity. Only our Creator knows whether a new cycle will begin after that. This great pattern of returning to the source or starting point is repeated in cycles of existence throughout the Universe. The symbol for this is the circle.

The Law of Universal Sympathy

This law concerns a yogi power that allows a yogi, a person who is devoid of the ego, to transfer information or to influence others' minds. Since the yogi is devoid of ego, which would mean having all soul qualities, he would only use this power for the good of all concerned.

The Law of Vacuum

Nature tolerates no vacuum. This awareness indicates that energies create a vacuum behind them, and this vacuum draws forth other energies to fill it. When beings move towards the Light, when they move toward higher spiritual dimensions, or move toward higher levels of consciousness, they create a vacuum. This vacuum in turn attracts others to fill the void left behind. In this manner when some progress toward higher levels of awareness, others are drawn toward higher levels of awareness. This law works on our earth plane, versus the law of Fulfillment which is for the level of the Hierarchy.

The Law of Vibration

This is the atomic law of the Solar System, one of the seven laws of the Solar System, also referred to as the law of Fire and is the basic law of evolution. All is rhythm and movement and when all that evolves on each plane attains the vibration of the atomic sub plane the goal is reached. The law of Vibration is the law of progress, of movement and of rotation. On the seventh or lowest plane, the vibration is slow, clogged and lethargic from the standpoint of the first, and it is in learning to vibrate or to rotate more rapidly, that we mount the path of return. It therefore involves building a finer matter of the form. All vehicles, the physical and psychic, astral, mental, buddhic and atmic, have all to be purified and refined.

The aim of the evolution for us is love dominated by intelligence or intelligence dominated by love for the interaction to be complete. The law of Vibration states that any vibration which is sent out for good, for service, increases into higher frequencies as it moves through space, until it returns to its origin, bringing the gifts of those higher frequencies back to the sender. Forces drawing on vibration for selfish purposes such as lust, power, greed, decrease vibrations in their frequency level. When beings send out selfish energies, those energies bring back, as magnets the lower vibrational forces the drawing of energy, decreasing the vibratory rate. On the other hand, radiance, the giving forth of energy and good deeds increase the vibratory rate. When beings radiate good, those energies increase into higher frequencies and bring back good. You can increase you vibration level through purifying your bodies of all negative energies, keeping a positive attitude towards life and by doing good deeds.

The universe is in a dynamic state. All forms vibrate and have energy. The higher the rate of vibration the greater the energy. All objects are composed of different arrangements of the same elementary particles and each has its own frequency and therefore its own amount of energy. The higher the energy level of a form the greater is the capacity to participate in higher life activities. Minerals, plants, animals and humans are all made of the same basic particles, the nature and the qualities of their lives differ because of their energy and vibration level.

Atoms always vibrate with such great rapidity that they seem motionless to the physical eye. At the other end of the scale are objects that vibrate so slowly that they also appear to be motionless or non-existent. In between are the various vibrations of living entities that range from consciousness all the way down to the lowly dust particle that plays an important role in the food chain. Still there are things even lower then dust. If we were to follow the scale of life all the way down to the utmost regions of the negative pole (undifferentiated matter), we again would find ourselves in the realm of spirit-the Alpha, and the Omega. All that is, begins in spirit and ends in spirit completing a single cycle of evolution that will be repeated countless numbers of times through eternity.

This law is of great importance to us now. The more we are able to raise our vibration level the more we are in tune with the natural laws of the cosmos and the more harmony we will experience in our life.

The Law of Will of God

The creators of our world carry out their work of form building under this law. God's working has to do with things free from change and movement—things divine. It is God's will that what is human should be divine and therefore all creation pushes forth to the God Light. God is all good and it is by reason of the good that all other things exist.

The Law of Will Power

This law concerns the individual divine within a soul extension personality projected from the complete entity. The individual developing soul extension differs in degree of will power from its other extensions soul family members. Depending on the conditions of an incarnational experience and the incoming will of this extension, the personality can possess a drive to accomplish something that may seem overwhelming to others in the soul family and/or other incarnational personalities friends. This law depicts the right and condition of each personality or soul extension to generate its own degree of will power.

The Law of Wisdom

Wisdom is the science of the spirit just as knowledge is the science of matter. While wisdom is synthetic and subjective, unites and blends knowledge is separative and objective, differentiates and divides. Wisdom is the enlightened application of knowledge through love, to the affairs of humanity. Wisdom has to do with the development and the progress of the spirit within the physical form and the expansion of consciousness through the many life times.

The wisdom of the triad exists for the use of the personality but it is barred by the lower mind. Only when the three meet through the regulation of the middle fire of the mind can a full light be achieved and the whole body be full of light. The fire from above, the higher self, and the fire from lower self, the kundalini, and the fire of the cosmic. In their union comes the burning away of all that hinders the completed emancipation.

Margo Kirtikar Ph.D.

The Soul's Journey

As the soul decides to take the path of human life it commits itself to leave the spiritual home, that of unity, and to embark on a journey of reincarnations on the physical plane, a world of duality and separateness. Our present reality in physical form on earth is but one phase of our complete human journey. Our purpose here on earth is to develop and strengthen our human qualities under conditions that are not possible on the spiritual plane. The spirit can only manifest itself through the material form. Our life on earth is a school where all souls go through a learning and a training process. The challenge is for us to be completely involved in the material world, at the same time we are supposed to remember. We are meant to remember our spiritual identity, to remember that we are a part of the Universal Soul and to remember our origin.

On earth our soul is given the use of a temporary form so that we can operate on the physical level. We refer to the physical body as the temple of the soul. Our first responsibility therefore, is to take care of our physical body in all its aspects. Through our relationships and experiences in each lifetime, as we go through the wheel of reincarnation, we are meant to acquire, to improve and to refine such positive human qualities as love, tolerance, patience, compassion, understanding, strength, intelligence, generosity, kindness and all other irrefutable soul qualities. In the Sufi tradition the ones who know say that God or Allah has three thousand names: one thousand he has revealed to His angels, one thousand He has revealed to His prophets; three hundred are to be found in the psalms of David; three hundred are in the Torah; three hundred are in the Gospel; ninety nine are in the Holy Qur'an. One, the name of His Essence, He has kept for Himself and hidden in the Qur'an. These names are also to be found in the qualities of the refined soul.

Life is all about energy and all relationships and interactions are essentially exchanges of energies. Through our physical body we exchange energy with material objects, humans, animals, plants and nature. We exchange energies on the physical level, emotional, mental and psychic level all of which help us to connect and to understand our relationships and interactions as we go through our individual lives. Our interpretations differ and our responses differ according to our human qualities. The test is for us to gain self awareness and our own identity so that we become masters of our lower sensations and feelings. While doing that we are required to constantly remember who we are and the spiritual world that we come from. The more we are able to remember and the more we are able to connect to the Source, the Universal Soul, the Universal Mind, the more infinite knowledge we have and the more inner harmony is experienced. Some of us experience all this without actually being aware of it, i.e. climb the ladder of evolution slowly without awareness, however, to evolve with awareness enables one to achieve greater things.

It is futile to compare or to complain about the injustice and the chaos in our world. We, individually and collectively, create our world every day anew. We are each responsible for our thoughts and our actions. In accordance with the unwritten universal laws of life we must accept the consequences, we pay the price according to our follies and we are rewarded when we have learned well and passed the tests that life imposes upon us. The law of Justice sees to that. The rules of 'the game of life' are fair because we are given a possibility to be forgiven and there is mercy and even 'grace' as an extra bonus. This means we are always given the chance to repent and to make amends if we wish it. By changing our mind, our beliefs and our actions we can lessen the burden that we carry or we can sometimes even clean the slate altogether.

In other words, by feeling remorse, we can change or erase our karma completely. The choice is ours to make. One thing is certain that millions of people have made the same experience. We know this because throughout the ages they have written about it and some of us know this to be the truth because we ourselves, have experienced what they are talking about. The moment you decide to repent and to ask for forgiveness, surrendering yourself totally in humbleness to the Higher Power, you feel, as if you have been touched by a fairy wand, flooded with light, you feel immediate relief. You go through a major transformation in consciousness and your life takes a turn to the better instantaneously. It makes no difference what belief you have, what status or what religion you belong to or how evil you have been. There are many thousands who have experienced this truth in their lives.

Whether you call the Higher Power, the Logos, the Absolute, the Essence, Sun, Light, Energy, Allah or God makes absolutely no difference because all are ONE and the same.

Afterword

One way to use this book after you have read it completely through at least once to familiarize yourself with the general idea, is to open it any time you feel like it, anywhere, at random and read one universal law. Any law. Read it slowly, get familiar with it, digest it and let the meaning of the law sink in to you. That you do by reflecting on it and thinking about it for one week or longer, any time anywhere. You will find that the more you concentrate on the law and its true meaning the more it will grow on you and the more you will understand. The next thing to do is to try to integrate the qualities of this law into your lifestyle while observing the law being activated by people around you. Continue to do this for a few weeks and observe how awareness of a particular law affects you and your life. Repeat this any time you feel like it with another law and then integrate that in addition to the first into your life. Repeat again with another law. You will find that if you keep the Noble Eightfold Path of Buddha constantly in your mind you would be activating many of these universal laws automatically.

Another way for you to use this book most effectively is when you are faced with a problem that you cannot solve. Look for one law that relates best to your problem, read it and reflect on the law and analyze your own thoughts and actions, try to figure out where you might have gone wrong and what you can do to put things right. Your life is guaranteed to take a turn for the better once you have learned to recognize and accept the energies of these universal laws and then to activate them with full awareness by integrating them in your way of life.

With your understanding of the universal laws you can activate the energies according to your individual experiences and situations. The importance is not the law in its naked version but in its living form. It is something that enables you to enrich yourself rather than impoverish or limit you. It is meant to expand your horizon. Think of universal laws as the elements of rain, vapor, steam, river or spring all of which is water manifesting in different forms with different qualities serving different purposes.

Perhaps now that we have a better understanding of these natural laws we can understand why good ultimately always triumphs over evil. We can understand that any totalitarian regime that limit and reduce its subjects to mechanical robots, robbing them of all their individualism and dignity is inevitably doomed to failure. We can understand that although the selfish and the greedy seem to be winning for a certain time, in the end live to regret and see their deeds boomerang on them in one way or another as are all dictators ultimately doomed to fall.

Humanity in general is becoming more aware. Thanks to modern technology, information and education is reaching out to the far and forgotten corners of the world. In particular we are learning more and more about our origin as humans, we are learning more than ever before about our own make up and our psyche. We also have more knowledge than ever before about our universe and what role our earth and we the human family play in this grand symphony of life. As ignorance diminishes along with the old political, educational and religious institutions, there is hope that the younger generations will make this a better world.

This book is not intended as a book of instructions for you to follow blindly, nor do I claim what I have written here to be the ultimate and only truth. My intention is rather to inspire you, to challenge and to activate your imagination, to prompt your own inner personal dialogue, to rouse your curiosity and to intensify your enthusiasm for the joy of life.

I would like to quote the following by C.G. Jung: "It is always the human being who interprets and gives meaning to any fact. We are susceptible to those suggestions with which we are already secretly in accord. For it all depends on how we look at things and not how things really are in themselves. A certain kind of behavior brings corresponding results, and the subjective understanding of these results give rise to the experiences which in turn influence behavior and thus close the circle of an individual's destiny.

Whoever protects himself against what is new and strange and thereby regresses to the past falls into the same neurotic conditions as the man who identifies himself with the new and runs away from the past. The only difference is that the one has estranged himself from the past and the other from the future. In principle both are doing the same thing. They are salvaging a narrow state of consciousness. The alternative is to shatter it with the tension inherent in the play of opposites in the dualistic stage and thereby to build up a state of wider and higher consciousness." C.G. Jung, Modern Man in Search of a Soul, pp. 96.

Margo Kirtikar Ph.D.

Glossary

Ascended Masters —

Also known as Avatars. They are beings who have all without exception gone through the incarnation process of life on earth, evolving through many lives with the same experiences of sufferings, joys and all the trials of the physical plane progressing to the highest levels until ascension to the higher planes of existence is achieved. Krishna, Moses, Jesus, Buddha are examples of the more widely known Masters. There are several many more who are less widely known to us.

Avatars/Masters —

An Avatar also referred to as Master is a highly evolved Being who is capable of reflecting some cosmic Principle or Divine quality and energy which will produce a desired effect upon humanity evoking a reaction and producing a needed stimulation. This energy is always focused through a manifesting Entity, is called forth by a demand or massed appeal and evokes response and consequent changes. The constant task of an Avatar is to establish nucleus of energy, spiritually positive. This for the Avatar is the anchoring energy. He focuses or anchors a dynamic truth, a potent thought form or a vortex of attractive energy in the three worlds of human living, which as the centuries pass, acts increasingly as a transmitter of divine energy which produces effects on human civilization. Christ, for example, anchored, 2000 years ago a nucleus of the energy of love.

Chohan —

"Lord," superior chief, divine or human.

Hierarchy —

A body of dedicated liberated units of life (Masters), in the fifth kingdom governed by Sirius, working in group formation with all forms and lives in all kingdoms and with all souls in particular. Its emphasis is on the consciousness aspect of all forms and expresses itself through the minds of all humanitarians, all aspirants, all disciples and all initiates. The Hierarchy can also express itself through the medium of thought currents and through them impose its concepts upon the embryonic minds of the general and average public. It also directs the educational work of all nations, so that the undeveloped masses can become in turn the intelligent general public. Hierarchy has three departments: the Manu, the Christ, the Mahachohan; the race of men, human beings have three expressions: the monad, the soul and the personality. Hierarchy is something that exists throughout nature. Everything in nature is ordered according to a hierarchical scheme.

I am Presence —

A radiant beautiful glorious body of light. Teachings by the Master St. Germaine who also introduced the Violet Consuming Flame which one can use to purify the physical, emotional and mental bodies. The 'I am Presence' is the Higher Self and can be contacted at will to protect one or to guide one. A positive attitude towards life, respect and harmlessness to all alike is mandatory.

Initiate—

An initiate is an enlightened evolved individual, initiated in the secret knowledge of the universe. An initiate pursues esoteric knowledge and goes through inner transformations with prayers and meditations, studies and practices. An initiate lives through victory over the lower nature and personality. An initiate's weapons are love and light.

Logos—

Manifested deity, the living expression of divine thought.

Man—

The word 'man' is actually a sanskrit word meaning 'thinking being' and refers to both male and female alike.

Monad—

I 'One' 'Unit' Indivisible, spark, divine center of every living being, atomic to cosmic.

Occult—

Concealed, obscured by something else as in astronomy. The word occult comes from the Latin word 'occultus'. The dictionary definition is: not divulged, secret, dealing with, knowledgeable in supernatural influences. Many practices are considered occult for example astrology, divination, the act of foretelling the future, magic and medium, a person thought to have powers of communicating with the spirits of the dead. Omen-any phenomenon supposed to predict good or evil. Sorcery, the use of supernatural power over others, witchcraft and wizardry.

Today practicing the occult has grown in acceptance and popularity. Only the names have changed. For example, instead of referring to persons who contact the dead as a medium, we call them channelers. Instead of using the term 'divination' we use the word 'psychic'. A mystic is someone who has blind faith in the supernatural and an occultist is someone who goes further than belief and studies supernatural energies. An Occultist is a truth seeker, adept in hidden wisdom and knowledge.

Sirius—

Sirius is known as the 'Dog Star' and is about 8.6 light years from earth. It is over 20 times brighter than our sun and over twice as massive. Even during normal phases of its life, a tremendous amount of electrical energy is created on Sirius, making it the most energized positive point in our little corner of space. In 1862 Sirius was discovered to be a binary star system with a companion star, Sirius B, which is 10'000 times dimmer than the bright primary, Sirius A. Every 49.9 years the 2 stars in the system, Sirius A and B come as close together as their orbits allow, creating huge magnetic storms between them. As they approach each other the stars begin to spin faster generating billions of volts of electricity. This energy is eventually released to flow down the magnetic field lines to the Sun which transmits it like a lens to all the planets. Sirius the 'dog star' stands for the 'spirit of wisdom' in the Zoroastrian tradition. Many reliable psychics and mystics firmly believe in the idea of a special gene, or personalized 'time capsule' programmed with the knowledge of the 'old ones' who came from the Sirius system centuries ago. This gene has been passed down from generation to generation to the present day. From this Sirian genetic strain a new school of magic has emerged.

Sirius was the guardian star of Egypt, its rising greatly affecting the life of everyday folk through the yearly inundation from the Nile. The earliest Egyptians believed Sirius was the home of departed souls. They considered Sirius to be the most important star in the sky, was astronomically the foundation of their entire religious system. The celestial movements determined the Egyptian calendar. Ancient Egyptians called Sirius the 'dog star', after the god Osiris, whose head in pictograms resembled that of a dog. It is said that Sirians helped build the great pyramids and temples of Egypt. They also helped to build many of the tunnels and pathways of the inner earth.

According to one Master Djwal Khul, Sirius is one of the more advanced training centers, or universities to which ascended masters travel. Sirians are a group consciousness of both physical and non physical nature. The Sirians in their etheric form are now working with many of us on earth giving us hints and conscious understanding of what our purpose is in the transformation of planet earth. The ascension will be a key, opening and integrating the light body with the physical, emotional and mental bodies, allowing each individual greater access to higher dimensions and experiences of oneness with others. Humans were meant to share in this role of caring for the earth and all of life on it, but most humans have been 'asleep' for a very long time now and are rapidly destroying themselves as well as earth and nature. The Sirians along with many others are here to help us change that.

Spiritus Mundi—

The universal Spirit all around us in space and around everything and in every being.

The Noble Eightfold Path —

Right view, right aspiration, right speech, right action, right livelihood, right effort, right mindfulness and right concentration. It is about having knowledge of suffering and the path leading to cessation of suffering. It is about understanding that everything physical is temporary. It is having aspiration for harmlessness, refraining from lying, hurtful speech and criticism. It is about refraining from violence, from taking what is not given and recognizing the golden middle line. It is having the right mode of livelihood in simple words doing honest work. It is about putting the right effort generating good deeds. Nothing comes from nothing. It is about being focused and one minded. The eightfold path is about meditating about life and being aloof from the pleasures of the five senses and activating the Divine in you.

The Seven Major Chakras —

(1) The crown chakra is the link to the spiritual world, through the pineal gland, energies affect the brain and rest of the body. (2) The brow chakra or the Ajna center is the link to the soul, it oversees all chakras below, balances mind and mental reason. It is linked to the pituitary gland, affects nerves, head, brain, eyes and face. (3) The throat chakra represents the ability to communicate and express oneself. True expression of the soul affects organs of throat, thyroid, parathyroid, glands, neck, nose, mouth, teeth and ears. (4) The heart chakra is the seat of the soul, gives the inner guidance for higher emotions, true love and friendship, compassion linked with the thymus gland, the energies of this chakra affect lungs, chest, upper back and arms. (5) The Solar Plexus chakra energies is the mind and personal will, lower emotions based on fear, anxiety, anger, jealousy, envy, insecurity. Here is the link between mind and

emotions is created and the energies affect the pancreas, liver, gall bladder and diaphragm. (6) The sacral chakra or hip chakra, is the seat for creativity and sexuality, here is the seat of joy and inner child. This is linked to sex organs, womb, kidneys, lower back and lower digestive organs. (7) The root chakra is the grounding, linked to planet earth. All issues of a physical nature, body, the five senses, sensuality, sex survival, aggression and self defense, affects endrocine glands system, adrenal glands, hips, legs and feet.

Third Dimension—

Our physical existence is on the third dimension, the soul and intuition plane is the fourth dimension, the Ascended Masters are on the fifth dimension.

Margo Kirtikar Ph.D.

Bibliography

I have omitted making detailed foot notes throughout this book as Cosmic and Universal Laws are part of mankind's heritage, belong to everyone who aspires for spiritual and psychic knowledge and cannot be attributed to any one person in particular. This book is the result of over ten years of extensive research and collecting of information from hundreds of esoteric books and manuscripts plus years of intensive study, observation and personal life experience. Sometimes having no choice, I have had to use exact esoteric definitions, more often I have interpreted the law from my point of view to make it understandable and accessible with practical suggestions for daily use. I do not claim that my work completely covers this complex and endless theme as there is much more that we know nothing about. Underneath is a detailed list of some of my sources. I would like to encourage you to make your own personal experiences and to make up your own mind.

Books by Alice A. Bailey, Lucis Publishing Company, London, U.K.
    A Treatise on Cosmic Fire
    The Consciousness of the Atom
    Initiation, Human and Solar
    Letters on Occult Meditation
    The Light of the Soul, Pantajali
    A Treatise on White magic
    Discipleship in the New Age, Vol, I and II
    The Externalization of the Hierarchy
    A Treatise on the Seven Rays
    Esoteric Psychology, Vol, I, II, III
    Esoteric Healing, Vol. IV
    Rays and Initiations, Vol. V

Margo Kirtikar Ph.D.

Books by Nicholas and Helena Roerich, Agni Yoga Society Inc., New York, USA.
    Agni Yoga 1929
    Infinity I 1930
    Infinity II 1930
    Hierarchy 1931
    Fiery World I 1933
    Fiery World II 1934
    Fiery World III 1935
    AUM 1936

Books by Omraan Mikhael Aicanhov, Editions Prosveta SA, Cedex, France
    Toward a Solar Civilization
    Man Master of his Destiny
    The Powers of Thought
    The Book of Divine Magic
    Looking into the Invisible
    Creation Artistic and Spritual
    Man's Psychic Life: Elements and Structures
    True Alchemy or the Quest for Perfection
    Man's Subtle Bodies and Centers
    The Symbolic Language of Geometrical Figures
    The Living Book of Nature

ECKANKAR-Mahanta Transcripts, The Spiritual Laws of Eck
The Bahai Faith
HUNAs Traditions Hawaii
Rudolph Steiner Books

St. Germaine Book Series (Mr. and Mrs. Guy W. Ballard) Vol. 1 to Vol.XII.

H.P.Blavatsky, (The Theosophical Publishing Co.Ltd. New York. USA.)
The Secret Doctrine, Vol. I and II.
Isis Unveiled Vol. I and II.

The Bhagavad Gita, The Gospel of the Lord Shri Krishna, Shri Purohit Swami, (Vintage Books, New York, USA.)
The Mahabharata, William Buck, Nal Penguin Inc. New York, USA.
The Kama Sutra of Vatsyayana, Richard Burton, (E.P. Dutton & Co.Inc. New York, USA.)
Inana Yoga, The Yoga of Knowledge, Swami Vivekananda, (Advaita Ashrama, Calcutta, India.)
The Vedas
The Teaching of Buddha, Bukkyo Dendo Kyoki, (Kosaido Printing Co.Ltd., Tokyo, Japan.)
Lectures on the Sutra, Hobenand Juryo Chapters, (Nichiren Shoshu International, Tokyo, Japan.)

The Holy Qur'an, Abdullah Yusuf Ali, (Amana Corporation, Brentwood, Maryland, USA.)
Islam in the World, Malise Ruthven, (Penguin Books, London, UK.)
The Most Beautiful Names, Sheikh Tosun Bayrak al Jarrahi al Halveti, (Threshold Books, Vermont, USA.)
Jesus in the Quran, Geoffrey Parrinder, (Oneworld Publications, Rockport, MA, USA.)

Judaism by Milton Steinberg, (A Harvest HBJ Book, London, UK)

Our Religions, Arvind Sharma, Harper Collins, San Francisco, USA.
The Dead Sea Scrolls uncovered, Robert Eisenman and Michael Wise, (Element Books Limited, Dorset, UK.)
The Holy Bible, Old and New Testament
Schöpfung im Wort, Friedrich Weinreb, (Thaurus Verlag, Weiler im Allgau, Deutschland.)(Roots of the Bible.)
The Egyptian Book of the Dead, E.A. Wallis Budge, (Dover Publications Inc., New York, USA.)
Tales from the Arabian Nights selected from the Thousand Nights and a Night, Richard Burton, (Avenel, Books, New York, USA.)
Make Your Life Worthwhile, by Emmet Fox, (Harper & Row, USA.)

About the Author

Margo Kirtikar, Ph.D.

Margo, a global citizen, has lived, studied and worked in the Middle East, Europe and the United States. She has three daughters and one grandson. She is an avid believer in continued adult education, self transformation and the refinement of the Self. Margo has a BA in Business and Economics, degrees in Leadership, Management, Banking, Psychology and Eastern healing techniques, and a BA, MSC and PhD in Metaphysics. She is also an accomplished artist. As an entrepreneur for over 25 years she pursued a career in international business and for the past ten years she has helped many through coaching, counseling in transpersonal psychology and spiritual healing.

It is not surprising that the metaphysical world and spirituality is a very real, natural and integrated part of her life as her origin is both Syrian and Indian. Margo grew up in Iraq, Syria and India with traditional but liberal parents and was since her childhood exposed to many religions and cultures. Today she is both a Swiss and a US citizen. Margo currently lives in Zurich, lectures, gives workshops and coaches individuals in consciousness expansion. She is an author of articles and books on self development and spirituality. Her first book on 'Change' was published in 1995. 'Visions Unusual' her second book, is on humanity as a family, developing the intangible sixth and the seventh senses, the mind and intuition. 'Flowing with Universal Laws' is her third book and focuses on soul qualities as one flows with universal energies.

Contact—

Margo Kirtikar Ph.D.
Seefeldstrasse 34
8008 Zurich
Switzerland
email: margo@visionsunusual.com
www.visionsunusual.com

Made in the USA
Lexington, KY
17 October 2010